The Viking Wars of Alfred the Great

Campaign Chronicles

The Viking Wars
of
Alfred the Great

Paul Hill

Campaign Chronicles
Series Editor

Christopher Summerville

Pen & Sword
MILITARY

First published in Great Britain in 2008 by
Pen & Sword Military
an imprint of
Pen & Sword Books Ltd
47 Church Street
Barnsley
South Yorkshire
S70 2AS

Copyright © Paul Hill 2008
Maps © Paul Hill and Christopher Summerville 2008

ISBN 978 1 84415 758 7

A CIP catalogue record for this book is
available from the British Library.

Typeset in Linotype Centennial
by Phoenix Typesetting, Auldgirth, Dumfriesshire

Printed and bound in England
by Biddles Ltd, King's Lynn

Pen & Sword Books Ltd incorporates the imprints of Pen & Sword
Aviation, Pen & Sword Family History, Pen & Sword Maritime,
Pen & Sword Military, Wharncliffe Local History, Pen & Sword Select,
Pen & Sword Military Classics, Leo Cooper, Remember When,
Seaforth Publishing and Frontline Publishing.

For a complete list of Pen & Sword titles please contact
PEN & SWORD BOOKS LIMITED
47 Church Street, Barnsley, South Yorkshire, S70 2AS, England
E-mail: enquiries@pen-and-sword.co.uk
Website: www.pen-and-sword.co.uk

Contents

The Viking Wars of Alfred the Great

Contents

List of Maps, Dynastic Chart and Plates

List of Maps, Dynastic Chart and Plates

Neere unto this, Eastward lieth Edinton, in old time *Eathandune*, where King Alfred in as memorable a battell as any time else, most fortunatly vanquished the bold, insolent and outragious Danes, and drave them to this hard passe, that they swore in set forme of oath forthwith to depart out of England.

William Camden

NINTH-CENTURY ENGLAND

- - - - Welsh border
ꙟ ꙟ ꙟ Marshes
▲ ▲ ▲ Forest

N

0   50   100
         Miles

Lindisfarne

NORTH SEA

Tyne

Durham •

Whitby •

I. of MAN

Ouse

• York

IRISH SEA

R. Humber

Anglesey

• Chester

Trent

• Lincoln

The Wash

Nottingham •
Derby •

The Fens

Peterborough •

Ouse

Thetford

Severn

Worcester •

Bedford •

• Cambridge

Gloucester •

• Oxford

Colchester •

London •

Reading •

Thames

Sheppey

Thanet

Winchester •

Wealden Forest

Dover

Exeter •

I. of WIGHT

ENGLISH CHANNEL

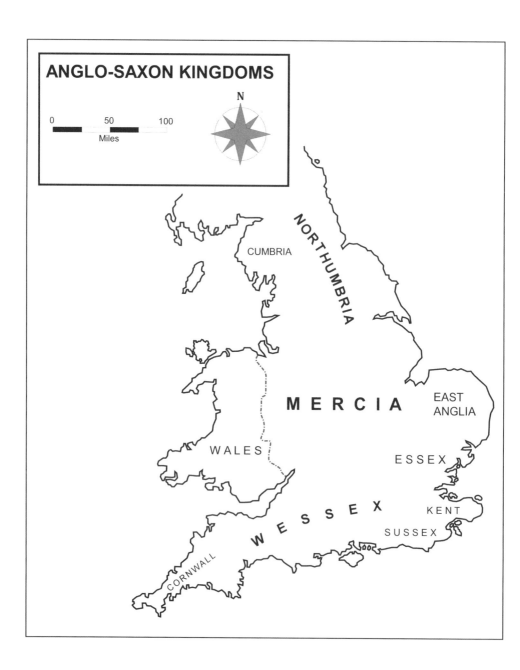

ANGLO-SAXON KINGDOMS

0   50   100
Miles

N

CUMBRIA

NORTHUMBRIA

MERCIA

EAST ANGLIA

WALES

ESSEX

WESSEX

KENT

SUSSEX

CORNWALL

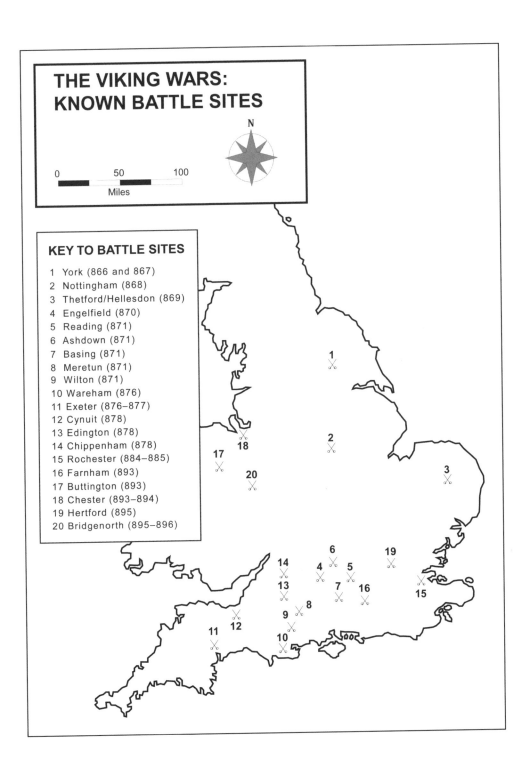

THE VIKING WARS: KNOWN BATTLE SITES

N

```
0        50        100
         Miles
```

KEY TO BATTLE SITES

1 York (866 and 867)
2 Nottingham (868)
3 Thetford/Hellesdon (869)
4 Engelfield (870)
5 Reading (871)
6 Ashdown (871)
7 Basing (871)
8 Meretun (871)
9 Wilton (871)
10 Wareham (876)
11 Exeter (876–877)
12 Cynuit (878)
13 Edington (878)
14 Chippenham (878)
15 Rochester (884–885)
16 Farnham (893)
17 Buttington (893)
18 Chester (893–894)
19 Hertford (895)
20 Bridgenorth (895–896)

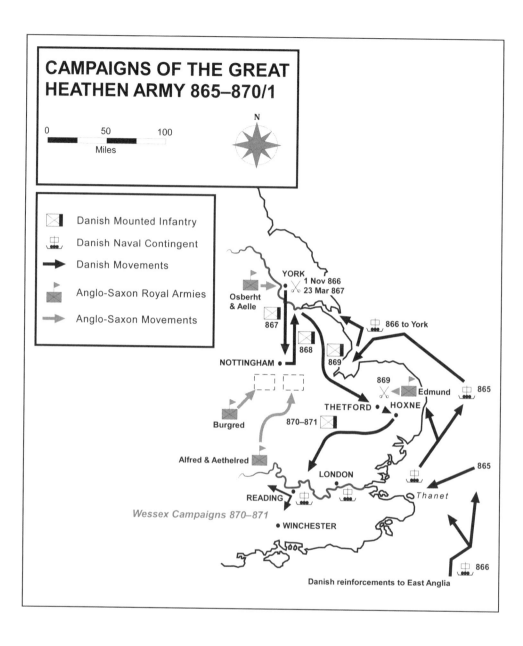

CAMPAIGNS OF THE GREAT HEATHEN ARMY 865–870/1

0 50 100
Miles

N

Danish Mounted Infantry

Danish Naval Contingent

Danish Movements

Anglo-Saxon Royal Armies

Anglo-Saxon Movements

YORK
1 Nov 866
23 Mar 867

Osberht & Aelle

867

866 to York

868

869

NOTTINGHAM

869

Edmund 865

THETFORD HOXNE

Burgred

870–871

Alfred & Aethelred

LONDON 865

READING

Wessex Campaigns 870–871

Thanet

WINCHESTER

866

Danish reinforcements to East Anglia

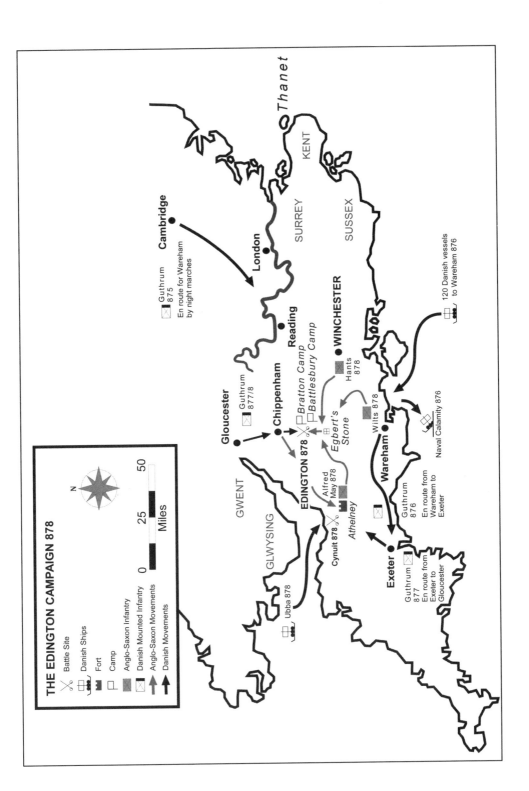

THE EDINGTON CAMPAIGN 878

Battle Site
Danish Ships
Fort
Camp
Anglo-Saxon Infantry
Danish Mounted Infantry
Anglo-Saxon Movements
Danish Movements

N

0   25   50
Miles

Thanet

KENT

SURREY

SUSSEX

Cambridge
Guthrum 875
En route for Wareham by night marches

London

Reading

WINCHESTER

Bratton Camp
Battlesbury Camp

Hants 878

120 Danish vessels to Wareham 876

Gloucester

Chippenham
Guthrum 877/8

EDINGTON 878
Egbert's Stone

Wilts 878

Alfred May 878

Athelney

Wareham
Guthrum 876
En route from Wareham to Exeter

Naval Calamity 876

GWENT

Cynuit 878

GLWYSING

Ubba 878

Exeter
Guthrum 877
En route from Exeter to Gloucester

Alfred's Family Background

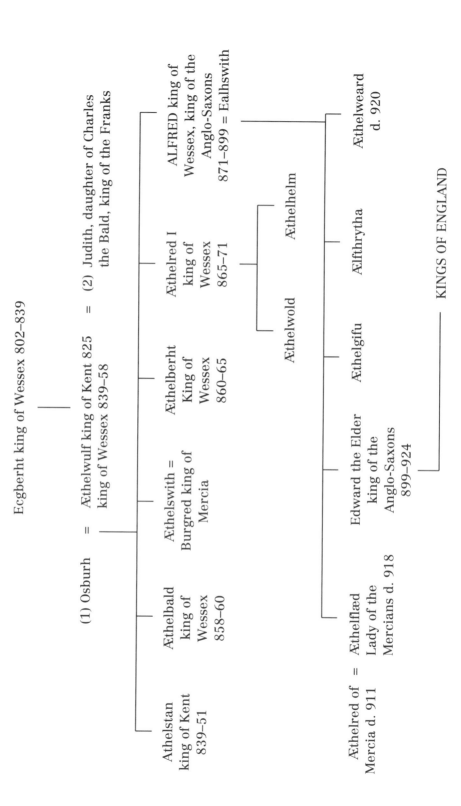

Ecgberht king of Wessex 802–839

|
Æthelwulf king of Kent 825 = (2) Judith, daughter of Charles
king of Wessex 839–58   the Bald, king of the Franks

(1) Osburh =

- Athelstan king of Kent 839–51
- Æthelbald king of Wessex 858–60
- Æthelswith = Burgred king of Mercia
- Æthelberht King of Wessex 860–65
- Æthelred I king of Wessex 865–71
  - Æthelwold
  - Æthelhelm
- ALFRED king of Wessex, king of the Anglo-Saxons 871–899 = Ealhswith

Æthelred of = Æthelflæd Lady of the
Mercia d. 911   Mercians d. 918

- Edward the Elder king of the Anglo-Saxons 899–924
- Æthelgifu
- Ælfthrytha
- Æthelweard d. 920

KINGS OF ENGLAND

Preface

‹─◦─›

That the ships lay there I had curious evidence some years ago. An old gentlemen, to whose politeness I am indebted told me that when the railway bridge across the fleet was being built, the navvies came upon many ships deep in the mud, several of which on exposure had evidently been burnt, as their charred remains showed. Indeed, about them lay numerous skeletons.

F.C.J. Spurrell

These are the words of enthusiastic archaeologist Flaxman Charles John Spurrell, who set out in 1879 to document what he could of the remains of a Viking camp at Shoeburyness in Essex. Spurrell was attempting to record for posterity the encampment of Hæsten, the great marauding Dane who invaded King Alfred the Great's (871–899) kingdom in the 890s, after years of successful campaigns abroad. As we shall see, what happened to Hæsten and his followers was markedly different from the fate of those Danes who had earlier infested the Anglo-Saxon kingdom of Wessex and nearly brought it to its knees. For now, a restored king was hard at work organising his territory into a carefully thought out system of fortifications, mobile armies and land workers. But as Mr Spurrell was setting out his tape measure over the banks and ditches that still remained at Shoebury, he was affected by the same wonderment that touches me. That camp was the centre of a tremendous struggle for power at the end of the ninth century.

The Viking Wars of Alfred the Great

Like Spurrell, I can imagine the cries of the women and children, the smell of the burning Danish ships. I can feel, too, the anger of a wronged king trying to defend his kingdom in the face of relentless foreign onslaught. These were days when a king's wishes were a matter of life and death for everyone involved in the working of the kingdom. Throughout this book, the reality of ninth-century warfare should become only too apparent. But who was this remarkable warrior-king and scholar, to whom so many historians in the English-speaking world have paid so much tribute?

Alfred grew up in a politically unstable world, in an age when the ancient Anglo-Saxon kingdom of Wessex was competing for supremacy among the heptarchy of kingdoms the Anglo-Saxons had established for themselves. The young Alfred could not have foreseen the great adventure he would ultimately embark upon; could not have imagined he would guide a war-torn people to a position of power and influence in lowland Britain. In the face of a series of potentially devastating foreign military threats, Alfred provided the platform for one of the greatest and most sustained military comebacks of medieval history. This *Campaign Chronicle* is a tale told looking forwards. Too much has been written about King Alfred over the centuries for any author to present the outcome of his wars as a surprise. But there are always areas for discussion and exploration in an era as obscure as the ninth century, and wherever that opportunity has presented itself, I hope I have taken it.

Alfred the Great is known to modern readers for countless worthy reasons. His political achievements have moved writers from his own times right up to our own, and his political legacy is still with the modern English people in a much-changed and much-threatened world. After his seminal victory at Edington in the spring of 878 – the battle around which this book is centred – Alfred was slowly able to realise a vision. He became, in a short time, the ruler not just of Wessex, but of that part of the country which incorporated the English remnants of the kingdom to the north of Wessex – Mercia. Into this enlarged kingdom, which took the name of the 'Kingdom of the Anglo-

Preface

Saxons', Alfred both imported and grew from within as many clerics, administrators, artists and advisors necessary to run a Christian kingdom. Though far from untroubled by further threats from fresh Danish invasions – and some duplicity from the old (now settled) foes – Alfred found enough time to concentrate on a healthy mixture of good governance and military provision. If the legends promoted in medieval and later times are to be believed, Alfred is the man responsible for the foundation of the Common Law, the establishment of the shires, the trial by jury system, the reordering of his military machine into a three-part system based on fort duties, mobile army service and land maintenance, the strategic building of fortified burhs (all within a day's march of each other) for the defence of his kingdom, and if all that was not enough, he is generally attributed with founding not just Oxford University, but the Royal Navy to boot.

Outstanding as these accomplishments are, the *Campaign Chronicles* series is concerned mainly with the military achievements of commanders, outlined in a blow-by-blow format. Here we are able, despite the great length of time passed, to piece together such a military chronicle. We owe the foresight of the king himself for such an approach, since it was he who instigated the recording of the *Anglo-Saxon Chronicle*, which covers his reign in detail. But there are other contemporary sources. The chronicler, Æthelweard, a tenth-century relative of the king, provides us with fascinating details on Alfred's campaigns, gleaned, it would seem, from a lost and more detailed version of the *Anglo-Saxon Chronicle*. Meanwhile, Irish, French and Scandinavian sources help paint a colourful picture of the exploits of the Danish armies of the era. In the case of the latter, despite some notoriously colourful story telling, we can glimpse the methodology and the psychology of the Viking.

Within these pages, we will attempt to answer the following questions: how did armies of the period function on the battlefield? How long did they take to assemble and deploy? Were there different types of units for different types of military job? To what use were horses put in these campaigns, which are

The Viking Wars of Alfred the Great

supposed to have been played out in an era before the adoption of true cavalry in England? How were the warriors equipped, and what were the tactics and strategies that won the day on the battlefields of ninth-century England? We also know Alfred overhauled many military systems for the better, and we will examine how these performed when under the ultimate test.

But this is a chronicle as much about the Danish armies as of the Anglo-Saxon. For years the Danes won the argument, both at a tactical level on the battlefield and at a strategic level in the countryside. The leaders of these Danish forces were responsible for the dismantling of all but one of the English kingdoms they attacked. They were bent on revenge, political domination and settlement, and brought with them the military muscle to back up their demands. To Anglo-Saxon eyes, these terrible and unholy northern warriors were bringing doom to their civilised world. No one had seen hosts of this size – and with this degree of intent – marching across their lands before. The world was changing.

And so, to the *Campaign Chronicle* itself. But we must start with the background in both England and Denmark. For if we are to understand the actions of Alfred and his great foe, Guthrum the Dane, then we must understand what went before. For therein lay the reasons why the antagonists first locked horns and how they behaved to one another. This much notwithstanding, a word of warning about the historical sources we rely upon is called for. All is not quite as it seems.

Background

⟫⟩-◦-⟨⟪

Hidden Messages from the Scriptorium

Throughout this book, a number of contemporary and near-contemporary sources are called upon to help us account for what happened during the wars of Alfred the Great. However, the sources most people rely upon in order to construct a narrative are not without their detractors over the years, and one in particular – perhaps the most valuable of them all – has had its authenticity called into question on more than one occasion.

When presenting evidence from these sources in this volume I have tried to read between the lines and explain any bias that I feel is hidden in the original texts, but there always remain some fascinating possibilities, whichever way we look at the stories that have come down to us.

In respect of two of our main sources, we are encumbered by the fact that we are not looking at them in anything like their original form. The tenth-century chronicler Æthelweard, whom we have mentioned above, and Alfred's biographer Asser, have provided us with material only known to us through the painstaking efforts of antiquarians and conscientious scholars of the early modern era. On Sunday, 23 October 1731, the Cottonian Library at Ashburnham House in Westminster, which housed so many valuable manuscripts variously retrieved after the dissolution of the monasteries, burned to the ground. Among the ashes were the unrecognisable remains of Asser's Latin *Life of King Alfred* and Æthelweard's *Latin* chronicle. Both authors had drawn heavily on the *Anglo-Saxon Chronicle*, initiated by the famous king himself, yet both these

The Viking Wars of Alfred the Great

writers had significant things to say from their own perspective. In the case of the latter, Æthelweard seems to have worked from his own copy of the *Anglo-Saxon Chronicle*, which contained additional information now lost to us. Many other valuable works were destroyed or nearly destroyed in the great fire at Ashburnham House that terrible day, but none so vital to our story as these two.

In the case of Asser, we must understand the nature of the controversy. The man certainly existed. He was discovered by King Alfred at a point in his reign when he was trying to rebuild the spiritual and intellectual life of a ravaged kingdom. He had come from St David's in Wales and was highly respected. But are we looking at his words when we survey the material we have available to us? Despite the Cottonian blaze, we are lucky in that Matthew Parker, the Archbishop of Canterbury (1559–1575), and the antiquarian, William Camden (1551–1623), who republished Parker's work in 1602, had both taken Asser's work and added to it the things they knew from other sources. So, into the story came the famous legend of Alfred burning the cakes and of Oxford University's claim to have been founded by the great king. To this we must add Francis Wise's frontispiece of Asser's *Life*, which was produced in 1722, and which very few people took notice of at the time.

Given then, that we are looking at Asser's work removed in time by several hands, it is surprising that so many historians have stuck with the general text of what he appears to say. There are some authentic sounding chimes about what we have: for example, the place names of England are also given in Welsh, consistent with a Welsh bishop who wrote in the knowledge that his countrymen would read his work. But Asser claimed to be a friend of Alfred and yet somehow struggles to get the year of his birth correct, and studiously avoids even giving the name of the king's wife. This has led some to suggest that the work Parker and Camden so diligently attended was in fact a later Anglo-Saxon forgery by a knowledgeable monk. The controversy will not rest and has been raging for a long time. For us, the material provided for the military aspects of Alfred's reign is fairly sound, whoever wrote the work. The author clearly used the *Anglo-Saxon Chronicle* as his guide and added some good information to aid the military historian.

As for Æthelweard, his tortured Latin syntax, and his own lineage are commented on as the pages of Alfred's story are turned in this book. Æthelweard was a fascinating character, whose presence on the stage of English history during the second age of Scandinavian incursions was nothing short of crucial.

But there are other, treacherous, writings. Scandinavian legend is packed with semi-legendary figures who may or may not have existed. Some are impossibly wrapped in legend, although others are far more palpable. Throughout this book, those figures whose actions appear in both legend and history are accounted for. Even some of the wilder flights of Scandinavian fancy are given room. The truth surrounding the motivations of the sons of Ragnar Lothbrok, who came to England in 865, may never be known. But what little we do know presents us with a fascinating story.

Lastly, one man deserves mention, but never gets it. Sir John Spelman (1594–1643), son of antiquarian Sir Henry Spelman (*c.* 1562–1641), is often viewed as one of Alfred's first early modern biographers. There is nothing particularly new in his work when we read it with the eye of a modern historian, but his words are often beautifully chosen. For that reason alone, I have included some material from his Latin work on the *Life of Alfred the Great*, which was translated into English with copious footnotes by Thomas Hearne in 1709.

For now, we must peer through the burning flames of Ashburnham House, to re-emerge hundreds of years earlier and step out of the hearth fires of Anglo-Saxon England, to examine what it was that made Alfred's world so vulnerable to the pagans from overseas.

Of Dynasties and Power

The English kingdoms the Danes ultimately dismembered all had a fault line running down the middle of them. Wessex, the sole survivor, was no exception. The dynamic behind early

The Viking Wars of Alfred the Great

medieval government was based around kinship, and in England, as well as elsewhere, the Germanic notion of the bond of lordship was the glue that stuck the social hierarchy together, and which, in theory, cemented the chief kinsman (or 'cyninge') to his throne. But here in England another factor was at work. It made its presence felt most keenly at succession time, when the power of one king was transferred to another. This was the witan.

An Anglo-Saxon witan was a council of wise men to whom the king would regularly turn for advice. It consisted of leading churchmen and secular lords, whose greatest collective power was in their ability to elect the successor to the king. Moreover, they could – as the West Saxon witan had done in 757 – deselect a king, too.

The ties of kinship could be divisive where there were competing families vying for the throne. In England there was nearly always a dynastic alternative to the incumbent. Put simply, if you were king, the secret to long-term success – over and above the destruction of your enemies and the successful protection of your people – was to stay in power long enough to secure succession, either for your son or your chosen heir. For this you will have to have played a masterful game of diplomacy with the witan. When kings obtained this right, and power did indeed pass from father to son or from brother to brother, the result was an accumulation of power, based on the expansion of the lordship ties that made everything work. But it was not until the tenth century, and the reigns of Alfred's son and grandsons in a greatly changed England, that this ideal became anything like a reality. While the tenth century proved that kinship could be a strength if managed properly, a great part of the ninth century proved the opposite. If you were the political enemy of an Anglo-Saxon king, all you had to do – but it was no easy task – was exploit the dynastic tensions at court and within the witan. This you could only do with the credible threat of force and as much intrigue as you could solicit. The Vikings were supreme masters at it, and we will explore how they did this to kingdom after kingdom. Perhaps it is worthwhile, however, to ask ourselves the one question that seems to

Background

have evaded many people over the years, and that is the question of who, exactly, the Vikings really were.

The Phenomenon of the Viking

To the churchmen of Europe they were the living embodiment of the prophecy of Jeremiah. It had been said that cruel men would rage out of the northern seas and visit harm on good people. With their bows and lances they would show no mercy. But in reality, the Scandinavians who plagued the kingdoms of the west in the eighth and ninth centuries were not so much a Divine punishment, as a mortal phenomenon resulting from certain political and social factors.

The word we use to describe these people is one shrouded in mystery, as arguments have raged over exactly what a Viking is. It was mooted by some scholars that the word might simply mean 'oarsman', and may be derived from a Scandinavian word used to describe the distance covered in an oarsman's shift. Others have suggested the word is derived from either the Old English, or closely related Old Frisian, word for a trading settlement or 'wic'. Such vulnerable coastal settlements were particularly popular with the raiders in the early years of the Viking era.

The Scandinavians themselves had a name for the marauders of the northern world, too. Their word 'Vikingr' meant 'Vik dweller', an inhabitant of the Viken area around the Oslo fjord in Norway. But it seems the word quickly took on the meaning of 'pirate' and was used to describe anyone who stepped outside mainstream society and decided to embark on a life of political opportunism and foreign adventure. In fact, the word 'wicenga' meant just that. You did not have to be a Dane or a Norwegian to be a pirate. But the Dane won the argument. Sir John Spelman, Alfred's first real biographer of the modern age, put it quite succinctly, set out here courtesy of Thomas Hearne's 1709 translation of his original Latin work:

And therefore from the Baltic Sea and other Maritime parts thereof so plentifully disburthened her self as that in England, as in the western parts of France and Spain.

5

The Viking Wars of Alfred the Great

The Countries to the coasts lay almost waste, by reason of the frequent incursions of Danes, Norwegians, Goths, Swedes, Frisons, and others that here promiscuously went by the name of Danes.

However, many of the people ranged against the Anglo-Saxons during Alfred's wars were, in fact, Scandinavian. To the French, much like the English, they were 'Northmen' or 'Danes'. To the Irish, who suffered greatly in these years, there was a distinguishable difference between the 'dark foreigner' (the Dane) and the 'fair foreigner' (the Norwegian). Generally, the nervous and pious scribes across Christendom collectively called the Vikings 'pagans'. As the years wore on, however, some Vikings – who were keen to establish political power in foreign lands – went as far as accepting baptism as a means to an end. As we shall see, this happened both in England and in Francia (sometimes referred to as 'Frankland' – the territory ruled by the Franks from the third century to the tenth century, roughly the equivalent of Modern France).

Some English chroniclers seem to be specific when they talk of the 'wicenga'. This is particularly the case when they were writing about raiding or piratical activity. In English culture it has become the practice over the centuries to use the word 'Viking' when discussing almost anything Scandinavian from the eighth to the twelfth centuries. Throughout this book, when we refer to the enemies of the Anglo-Saxons as represented by Halfdan, Ivarr, Ubba and Hæsten we will mainly use the term 'Danes', unless there is good evidence to suggest that, before us, we do in fact have a pirate of the seas.

As for Denmark itself, what was it that made a relatively well ruled and prosperous homeland give rise to the wandering people who, with their shallow draft vessels, would become the scourge of the western world and beyond? In the era immediately prior to the so-called Viking era, it is claimed that overpopulation in Scandinavia caused an exodus. Land-hunger, too, is cited as a reason. But land-hunger only truly existed along the western coast of Norway, a relatively thin fertile strip. Clearly, other dynamics were at work.

Background

First of all, trade had once again begun to flourish after a lull following the fall of the Western Roman Empire. With trade came an injection of a large amount of silver into the northern economies and the transportation of a whole load of portable wealth from the Baltic and the Mediterranean to the Atlantic coast. To the opportunistic pirate there was great plunder to be had. As the Frisians, Franks and Anglo-Saxons built their trading settlements at places such as Hamwih (Southampton), Lundenwic (London) and Quentovic (Boulogne), the sea traffic continued to rise. These settlements were vulnerable and low lying with no stout defences. Trading was often carried out not far from the beached ships, on the foreshore – an ideal target for passing Vikings. But this vulnerability does not explain why, by the time of King Alfred, there were so many Danish sails on the horizon off the coast of Wessex. This is explained by politics.

The Frankish empire had been strong under Charlemagne (742–814) and had, for the most part, been able to contain sporadic raiding. Frisian shipping dominated northern waters at this time. Charlemagne's son, Louis the Pious (814–840), granted land inside the empire to exiled royals when the Danish kingdom experienced problems, and from this time – as the Frankish kingdom started to disintegrate under Louis's sons and more Danes were brought into the military argument to support one claim or another – Danish interest in the politics of the west picked up.

Sources agree that raiding along the coast of England and Francia also increased around 834–835. Between 800–810 Denmark had been ruled by King Godfred, a powerful and centralising ruler, but when one of his retainers murdered him there was chaos. During the reign of Hemming (810–812) there was a war involving Godfred's sons. One of these, Horik I (813–854), rose to the fore and tried to stem Danish piratical activity in the northern seas. Horik even sent letters to Louis in Francia, assuring him he had ordered the capture and execution of Vikings who had attacked Walcheren and Dorestadt the previous year.

But there was still chaos and murderous intrigue in the halls of the Danish kingdom. In 854, not long before the great descent on England, an attack was led against the Danish king, which succeeded in killing the entire court – apart from one small boy – leading to a complete disintegration of the kingdom. There was now nothing to stop ambitious men striving for a new destiny, either at home or abroad. The fury of the Northmen was about to be unleashed.

The Early Raids in England

Here terrible portents came about over the land of Northumbria, and miserably frightened the people, these were immense flashes of lightning and fiery dragons were seen flying in the air. A great famine immediately followed these signs and a little after that in the same year [. . .] the raiding of Heathen men miserably devastated God's church in Lindisfarne island by looting and slaughter.

Anglo-Saxon Chronicle
(Peterborough Version E), entry for 793.

Beaduheard, the Portland port-reeve, cannot have known how he would make his contribution to English history. Nor, indeed, could he have imagined the price he would pay for it. Going about his usual business, he had been alerted to a trinity of sails on the horizon. If these vessels contained traders – perhaps from Frisia or Francia – then here was the chance to regulate and tax them, providing some income for King Beorhtric (786–802) of Wessex. If they were not merchants, then they must be ushered to the king at Dorchester, so they could account for themselves.

They were not merchants. Beaduheard was surprised and confused as to the origin of the strange men in their three ships, and he commanded them to accompany him and his small group of men to Dorchester. No such journey would be undertaken. The Vikings had arrived 'for the first time' in England. The shingle was soon stained red and Beaduheard never got the opportunity to report to his king. Nor did any

Background

West Saxon present. These three shiploads – described variously as 'Northmen' from Hordaland in Norway, or as 'Danes' – had, by a single act of barbarity, brought a biblical prophecy to life on the southern shores of England, as their kinsfolk would do to the community of Lindisfarne just four years later.

For the Christian chroniclers, the men who descended like 'stinging hornets' on Lindisfarne and elsewhere were sent by God as punishment for their sins. In fact, Alcuin (the greatest scholar of his age, who had left York for the service of the Emperor Charlemagne) wrote to Æthelred I, king of Northumbria (774–779 and 790–796), setting out the reasons why Lindisfarne had suffered. The 'luxurious habits' practiced in Northumbria had brought about the disaster, and as such, the raid 'was merited by some unheard-of evil practice'.

But if churchmen were taking an apocalyptic view, and looking at ways of modifying their moral behaviour to make the heathens go away, secular leaders in England were obliged to be more practical. King Offa of Mercia (757–796) had known of the pirate threat and made provision for it in the Mercian under-kingdom of Kent, by requiring fortress-building and bridge-repair as duties expected from his subjects. As early as 804 the community of Lyminge in Kent, under the guiding hand of their abbess, Selethryth, had managed to acquire a refuge for her followers within the old walls of Canterbury, instead of the exposed coastal site they had previously occupied. Kent seems to have suffered badly during these early years of the Viking era. The enemy even set up its own ditch-and-bank style fortifications on the shores of the ancient kingdom – a phenomenon noted by the Mercian King Ceolwulf (821–823), who reiterated an obligation to destroy such fortifications in a charter of a grant of land to Archbishop Wulfred in 823.

By the early ninth century, the kingdom of Wessex – long at loggerheads with the Mercians – had more or less overcome its old adversary. Alfred's grandfather, King Ecgberht (802–839), slowly gained the ascendancy after being exiled and facing all sorts of tribulations. He strove to extend West Saxon influence everywhere below the River Humber. In 815 he invaded Cornwall, in a campaign long remembered by the 'West Welsh' as they were then called. In 825 the people of Kent, Sussex, Surrey and Essex submitted to the West Saxon king, and at the same time, the East Angles petitioned the king for protection from their traditional enemies, the Mercians. That same year saw Ecgberht exploit dynastic tensions within Mercia by bringing King Beornwulf (823–825) to battle at Ellendun, near Swindon. By 829 the West Saxon king could claim to have realised a dream. When he took his army to the Dore, in Yorkshire, the traditional boundary zone between Mercia and Northumbria, he did so as a latter-day 'Bretwalda', vaunted as such by the *Anglo-Saxon Chronicle* – the wielder of the widest power in Britain. The Northumbrians submitted to him there and recognised his power, but it would be a long time, and under quite different circumstances, before any king from south of the Humber would be able to throw his weight around in the northern world.

For Æthelwulf (839–858), who had been a subking in Kent during the 830s, the dynastic weaknesses that characterised his father's exploitation of Mercia should have been a lesson to him, given what was to come. In Francia, too, the post-Charlemagne world was inevitably characterised by fraction and confusion in the wake of a remarkably successful reign. All this provided Vikings with the opportunity to play one party off against another, and to fill the gaps in regional power vacuums to such effect, they would eventually found a famous northern dukedom for themselves.

Thus it was not long before the Vikings poured forth on both sides of the English Channel. The trading settlement at Dorestadt, in Frisia, was raided in 835, and the Isle of Sheppey was deprived of its trading wealth and portable riches, which were stored in the royal nunnery there.

In England, the islands of Sheppey and Thanet would be used time and again by the enemies of the Anglo-Saxons. Not only did they provide a defensible position, but they allowed a range of options for movement. There was still the old Roman road network, which gave access to important and wealthy settlements, and by seas and rivers there was virtually nowhere in England the Vikings could not reach.

Background

But it was not just Kent that received the attention of the raiders. Around thirty vessels in 836 descended on the royal estate at Carhampton, in Somerset. This time an enemy was heading directly for a source of wealth other than a port – a sign that the Vikings were broadening their goals. King Ecgberht was obliged to respond to this threat, so he gathered the West Saxon fyrd as quickly as the antiquated system would allow, and headed out to Carhampton. When he got there, he was confronted with a ferocious enemy that knew how to fight and win. The resulting casualty list sent alarm bells ringing around the halls of Winchester. Two ealdormen and two bishops lay slaughtered in this, the great king's first encounter with a new Dark-Age menace.

Wessex Responds

The news of the defeat of the self-styled Bretwalda aroused passions across the island, none more so than in Cornwall, where the embarrassment of 815 lived large in the minds of the sons of those who suffered it. And so, when a Viking force landed in Cornwall in 838, it did not meet hostility from the natives, but was enticed by them to join forces against a common enemy. The combined force of Cornish and Viking warriors set about destroying West Saxon influence in that corner of the realm.

As Ecgberht got wind of the uprising, he summoned his army again and marched to Hingston, where he met both his foes, and this time delivered the knock-out blow previously denied him. Both his enemies fled the scene and left Ecgberht in charge of the battlefield. This grand old man, who had seen countless battles, who had spent three years in exile in Francia because of his dispute with the Mercians, must have cherished the moment. But he knew this most recent of enemies did not fear his God. He felt – as others felt – that these heathens were sent to punish him and his people. When he lay on his deathbed two years later, it remained to be seen whether the prophecy he had announced to Louis the Pious of Francia in a famous letter would come true. The old English king had told his counterpart that, because of the sins of the Christian peoples, this horror was being visited upon them all. He foretold a vision that if the Christians did not soon repent, a great heathen fleet would do for them all.

King Ecgberht was succeeded by his son Æthelwulf (839–856). A notoriously pious man, the new king was, nevertheless, no slouch when it came to warfare. As a devout Christian, however, he does seem to have had more than half an eye on the value of Rome in his life. At the time of Æthelwulf's accession, his eldest sons were at an appropriate age both to assist him in the governing of the realm and to interfere with his plans. One of them, Athelstan, received Kent, Surrey, Sussex and Essex, over which to rule. He would do his part in the fight against the pagan menace in the years to come.

The year 840, however, saw more grief for the West Saxon hierarchy. As Louis the Pious neared his death across the sea, and as the pagans – at large in Ireland – began to settle in for the winter, the signs for the Anglo-Saxons were not good. The Scandinavian threat was about to step up a gear. One brave West Saxon ealdorman named Wulfheard met a force of thirty-three shiploads of Vikings at Southampton and successfully defended the nearby trading settlement, achieving victory where others had so conspicuously failed before him. Wulfheard, who, as it happens, was close to death, could at least go to his grave safe in the knowledge he had done everything possible to safeguard the interests of his lord's kingdom. At any rate, sources say he died peacefully.

And yet, Ealdorman Æthelhelm was not so lucky. His was the misfortune to encounter a group of Danes who had landed further down the coast at Portland. He took the men of Dorset with him to confront the enemy, but sadly neither he nor his key followers would return. It was now happening everywhere along the coast of England. Ealdorman Hereberht of Kent was killed by a pirate force of 'heathen men' at Romney Marsh in 841. This same year, further victims are recorded along the Lincolnshire and East Anglian coasts, and once again in the long-suffering coastal hamlets of Kent.

The next year it was the turn of the vulnerable trading settle-

Background

ments on the estuaries of Francia and England. At the mouth of the Canche sat Quentovic, a thriving port that carried pottery, quern stones, luxury items and a significant amount of passenger traffic to England. It was ruthlessly sacked. So too was Rochester (situated probably at the end of a lucrative wine trade route) and the trading settlement at Lundenwic. As if this were not enough for the West Saxon leadership, the estate at Carhampton was once again targeted in 843 and this time thirty-five shiploads of pagans proved too much for Æthelwulf, just as they had done for Ecgberht.

For the next few years the *Anglo-Saxon Chronicle* is remarkably silent. That is not to say, however, the raids were not continuing. In fact, what little evidence we have points more to an escalation than a relaxation of military activity. We are reliant on the Continental source, the *Annals of St Bertin*, which tells us, in an enigmatic record for the year 844, that there was something approaching a titanic struggle between the forces of the Northmen and the Anglo-Saxons somewhere across the sea. It had been a battle that raged for three days, resulting in defeat for the Anglo-Saxons. The *Anglo-Saxon Chronicle*, however, picks up the thread again in 848 with a number of entries that might seem to herald the arrival of an upturn in West Saxon fortunes. In that year Ealdorman Eanwulf and his Somerset men, along with Ealdorman Osric and his Dorset men, fought at the mouth of the River Parret against a Viking force and won a surprise victory. Meanwhile, in the quiet royal estate at Wantage, a boy was born into this dark and dangerous world. It was the year 849. The fifth son of Æthelwulf was named Alfred. All Alfred's brothers were older than he, so it must have seemed unlikely to everyone at the West Saxon court that the young prince would ever inherit the throne himself. Alfred grew up attentive to the stories of the great trials of his brothers, but surely blissfully unaware of the vital role he would himself play in the years to come.

As he was being nursed and cared for at Wantage, the boy Alfred would have been too young to understand fully the elation at the news of Ealdorman Ceorl's great victory over

The Viking Wars of Alfred the Great

the pirates with the Devonshire fyrd in 851. His elder brothers, however, were in the thick of it that year. Athelstan of Kent (a shadowy figure who seems to have commanded some respect from contemporaries), accompanied by Ealhhere of Kent, attacked a great enemy fleet off the coast at Sandwich and managed, to their great credit, to capture nine of the enemy vessels while the remainder fled. But for all of Athelstan's efforts in Kentish waters, this was also the year in which, according to the *Anglo-Saxon Chronicle*, the Vikings first spent the winter on Thanet. If that was not enough to convince Athelstan and his father that their work was far from complete, then the arrival in the Thames estuary of a fleet of 350 vessels – a simply astounding number – will have more than impressed. The crews of this fleet were responsible for the sacking of Canterbury and London and must have seemed unstoppable.

The great Viking fleet, about which we know very little, came a long way inland up the Thames before turning north and engaging the forces of the Mercian King Beorhtwulf (*c.* 840–*c.* 852). The Mercian force was soundly defeated and its remnants scurried to their settlements, not knowing what the future might bring. The victorious Vikings turned south and crossed the river somewhere in Surrey, continuing south. Æthelwulf's Wessex was to be targeted for perhaps the second time by a colossal enemy force. On this occasion, however, the enemy had entered not the territory of a timid and unsure king, but had marched right into the wolf's lair. Wessex, frequently caught by surprise in recent years, had one redeeming characteristic seemingly not shared by others, namely, a remarkable tenacity. It was not Athelstan who met the enemy at a forgotten field in Surrey called Aclea, but the king himself, along with his son Æthelbald. Here they took on the whole enemy force in open battle, and whatever their tactics, they won a striking victory, the news of which travelled across the sea to faraway parts of Christendom. The jubilation must have been great: the enemies of Christ could be defeated after all.

Of course, such a victory was bound to make the West Saxon king popular. The new king of Mercia, Burgred (852–874), who

14

was mindful of the dwindling finances he had inherited and of the family rivalries throughout his kingdom, wisely came to Æthelwulf to ask for his aid in his campaigns against the rebellious Welsh king Rhodri Mawr in 853. Burgred did indeed receive help from Wessex, and Wales was, for the time being, subdued as far north as Anglesey. Although he was successful in his military campaigns that year, Burgred perhaps unwittingly began an association with Winchester that would all but do for the independent kingdom of Mercia in the long run. By the spring of that year, Alfred's sister Æthelswith was married to the Mercian king in a great ceremony at the royal estate at Chippenham – a place that would come to notice in less happy times a few years later.

Rome, Raids and Decimation

Nobody knows quite why the king sent his little and most loved boy to Rome. Nobody knows who took him there, although the pilgrims' party is likely to have been large. Perhaps the victory at Aclea had brought a significant peace and fame enough for Æthelwulf to convince himself of the need for papal blessing of his royal line. Alfred's older brothers were tied up with defending and governing the kingdom, so it seemed natural to place the future in the hands of the one who had so much ahead of him. But it is not clear if Alfred was the only son of Æthelwulf to take the momentous journey. Surviving records along the route point to his slightly older brother Æthelred also being present, and this would make a great deal of sense. Both these children were the sons of the mysterious Osburh, a royal lady who would soon disappear from English history as quickly as she appeared. She may well have been the mother of Alfred's older brothers, but Alfred and Æthelred represent a younger generation of the king's children. One thing is certain, however, the trip to Rome profoundly affected the young Alfred and in the long run had huge consequences for the whole of England. We might permit ourselves to imagine what a young boy thought of the decaying grandeur around him, what he made of Pope Leo IV's spectacular rebuilding of parts of the city, including the area around the Vatican Hill, which was now lined with state-of-the art defences, an area which became known as the Leonine City. From the ashes of the Saracen raids, one man had trusted in God and built himself a citadel. One boy had taken note.

While Alfred stood at the threshold of the holy Apostles, ready to receive a welcome which some argue amounted to a sort of investiture, the redoubtable Ealhhere of Kent, accompanied by Ealdorman Huda of Surrey, along with the men of that region, engaged an enemy fleet at Thanet. History records that their descent on the Vikings was successful at first, but too many men fell into the waters of the River Swale. At the bottom of the pile were two drowned ealdormen. Ealhhere and Huda had learned the hard way that attacking an enemy in a fortified position of its own choosing was not the way to win a war.

It was a year before the boys returned from Rome. Nothing on the scale of the disaster at Thanet is recorded before their homecoming. At Easter 854 a crowd of keen prelates and dignitaries gathered around the hearth at the hall in Wilton, asking question after question of the pilgrims. Ealhstan, the long-serving bishop of Sherborne – as keen with the sword as the crook – listened to stories of a journey that had taken the party through Frankish domains and Pavia to Rome. Swithin, the bishop of Winchester, whose place in Christian hagiography would itself soon be assured on account of his great piety, also listened intently. But if anyone had a heart more filled with passion than these two when hearing the tales of a young boy, it was the king himself.

Æthelwulf resolved to make his own pilgrimage to Rome. Making this decision was one thing, but working out how to persuade the witan and the Church to accept the arrangements he wished to make for government in his absence was quite another. The king's solution was radical to say the least. Before he set off 'across the sea to Rome' Æthelwulf gave one-tenth of his lands to the Church, prompting the phrase 'the decimation of Æthelwulf', coined to describe this monumental feat of gift giving. Administratively speaking, it was a major headache for the scribes employed in recording it, and its ramifications, in terms of land disputes, would rumble for centuries, with

Background

various people – both religious and secular – basing their claims to entitlements on this one single act. The year was now 855.

Having enticed the support of some of his nobles for his trip to Rome (employing the customary method of land giving), the king now needed to leave his kingdom in safe hands. Athelstan had by now died (sadly the sources do not say how) so the eldest son was Æthelbald. In much the same way as his own father had divided the kingdom with him, Æthelwulf gave to Æthelbald the best part of historic Wessex, while his other, slightly younger, son, Æthelberht, would rule over Kent, Surrey, Sussex and Essex. It is not unlikely that, as he set foot on the ship that would surely have carried him from Hamwih to Quentovic, the king of Wessex had with him the boy who had told him so much of Rome, his longed-for destination.

But the pilgrims left behind them a kingdom facing uncertainty. While they were away, a heathen fleet overwintered for the first time on Sheppey. Some sources say it even included Frisians among its number. News of this may not have reached the party, but when they finally got to Rome and prepared to enter the English quarter Pope Leo had prepared for them, the news they heard would not have pleased them: Leo was dead. Alfred, who had by now lost his mother Osburh, must have been distraught. The king now faced uncertainty even here in Rome, where the emperor Lothar had chosen an antipope, Anastatius, in preference to Pope Benedict, Leo's successor. Significant public disorder followed in Rome, witnessed, presumably, by Alfred and his father. Finally, papal legates managed to arrange a contest between the two candidates, in the form of an election, which Benedict won. It was one of many power battles between the emperor and the papacy and it showed that, for now at least, the emperor was losing the argument. Æthelwulf and his son gladly gave their gifts to the new Benedict III, but it is not known to what extent the Anglo-Saxon king had interfered with the papal succession crisis.

Something significant happened on the way back from Rome. Æthelwulf had perhaps long sought a union with Francia, and he went to the court of Charles the Bald (840–877) to finalise the details of his marriage to a young princess, Charles's daughter Judith. The difference in their ages was colossal. She was barley a teenager and he was around fifty years old. But this was a political union. In October 856 it became a political reality, as the young girl was married to the West Saxon monarch at Verberie, amid resplendent surroundings. But something else happened at Verberie. Judith was not only married by Hincmar of Rheims to the king of Wessex, she was also anointed as queen. The discomfort of the leading figures in the West Saxon party must have been palpable. Wessex had not allowed the wives of kings to rule as queens for a long time, and here they were expected to accept a child, with whom Charles the Bald intended Æthelwulf should rule Wessex.

The king returned to Wessex 'in good health', but he found things had changed. Æthelbald was reluctant to relinquish his hold on power and had gathered the support of Ealhstan, the bishop of Sherborne and the ealdorman of Somerset. Foremost in his mind would have been the threat presented by the prospect of his ageing father siring an heir or two in the next few years. An extraordinary arrangement then ensued, the details of which are unclear. Æthelbald seems to have kept much of the greater part of Wessex he had inherited during his father's absence and the old king was given the lands in Sussex, Kent, Essex and Surrey, over which his son Æthelberht had dutifully presided. This decision seems to have been made by the witan and was an attempt to avoid in Wessex the friction that had happened in Francia at the death of Charlemagne. Frankish sources do in fact hint that Æthelwulf retained control of his kingdom at this difficult time, but quite what Charles the Bald made of his daughter's new position at the wrong end of the kingdom is unclear. There is another interpretation, however. The old king probably still held sway in some parts of central Wessex, as well as in the east. To either side of him he had two sons: one in the west, harbouring dark thoughts against his father, and one still presiding over the lands of Athelstan in the east. Whichever interpretation is correct, it was clearly an uncomfortable time.

Background

All we know for sure is that the stand off between father and eldest son continued. By January 858 it seemed the kingdom would be permanently split into these eastern and western provinces, along the lines apparently sketched out in the old king's will. But in that month Æthelwulf died and is thought to have been buried in the church at Steyning in Sussex. It was now that Æthelbald (856–860) took an unpopular move by marrying his father's young widow. Now it would seem that Æthelbald took control over all that his father had after his return, plus that which he himself had been in charge of in the west. It all looked good for Æthelbald, as he sat with his queen, thinking of raising a dynasty with her. But he did not have time. The new king of Wessex died in 860 and Judith's sortie into Anglo-Saxon politics had come to an end. She would return to her father's side, across the water, and embark on another equally remarkable political life abroad.

The Legends Descend

While Bishop Ealhstan presided over the burial of Æthelbald at Sherborne, Æthelberht (860–865) moved with great speed to exact a coup and take for himself the whole of Wessex in a form that would have been recognisable to his grandfather, King Ecgberht. There are hints that Æthelberht's takeover was sanctioned by the witan. It is difficult to see how this could not have been the case. It was a time of crisis and one of the key functions of the witan, among other things, was crisis management. The young boys Alfred and Æthelred were promised their share would be restored to them, as they witnessed the witan making its decision.

But the temporary cancellation of Alfred's inheritance would have been only one of the things plaguing the mind of the youngster. The year 860 saw the arrival in England of an extraordinary campaigner from Scandinavian legend. His name was Weland. His army, or band of followers, had been with him in Francia, on the Somme, where they had hounded Charles the Bald at the same time as a huge force of Vikings, stationed on the isle of Oissel, were doing much the same thing in the middle of the River Seine. Charles, after attacking his own subjects who were brave enough to take on the invaders, then tried to play the two groups off against each other and failed conspicuously. Weland, who was willing to take the bribe to attack his counterparts on Oissel, grew impatient, and while he secured Frankish promises to give him the 3,000 pounds of silver he required for the job, he set sail for England.

To the Hampshire coast he came, and quickly his huge force of marauders fell upon the capital of Wessex and set it ablaze. Buoyed by their success, they spread inland as the bishop of Winchester surveyed the destruction of all that was good and Christian. It was a scene that must have haunted St Swithin until his death the following year.

But there then came a significant moment in the career of one notable Anglo-Saxon, who would return just when Wessex needed him. Weland had underestimated the West Saxon fyrd. Miles away from their ships – a classic Viking mistake – and loaded with booty, the Scandinavians were caught in the open by Ealdorman Osric of Hampshire, and the tenacious ealdorman of Berkshire, who shared his name with the late king of Wessex, Æthelwulf. The two ealdormen smashed their way into the invaders and deprived them of all they had gained. Losses on the Viking side were great in terms of men, but Weland survived it all. He returned to Francia and continued to terrorise Charles the Bald, but did indeed attack the Oissel Vikings and even managed to extract money from them. Soon Weland's career would end in death, after an extraordinary duel at the court of the Frankish king, but there were other characters sailing through northern waters during Æthelberht's reign, and their memory survived the Viking area in the form of semi-legend.

One of these figures, Hæsten, would meet with Alfred many years later. In 859 Hæsten had been campaigning in the Mediterranean with Bjorn Ironsides, a son of the celebrated Ragnar Lothbrok, a character who was – depending on which saga one consults – either two people, one person or nobody at all. Hæsten famously attacked Luna, in Italy, mistaking it for Rome, but returned to his base on the Loire laden with booty. Wessex was not yet his target, and he successfully meddled in

Background

Frankish politics (for personal gain) for many years to come.

Establishing the reality behind the legends of Ragnar Lothbrok and his sons is not possible. The mythology and the facts have been interchanged so often as to be indistinguishable. Ragnar may have held Paris to ransom in 845. He may also have been killed by King Ælle of Northumbria in 865, by being thrown into a pit of snakes, but this would not have been the first time he died, if legend is to be believed. One of his sons, Ivarr, appears to have been a menacing presence on the seas around England and Ireland at this time, terrorising the Irish in the late 850s. Soon Ivarr, whose sobriquet 'the boneless' has intrigued historians for generations, would fetch up on the shores of East Anglia with his brothers in an apparent bid to avenge the death of his father. It would be a visit that would change the history of a whole people.

With these great warriors and their followers marauding the waters of northern Europe, it is perhaps surprising that the reign of Æthelberht is so devoid of military action, save for the disaster at Winchester shortly after the accession and a raid on Kent at the end. To his credit, the king of a recently reunited Wessex did indeed protect the interests of the two younger brothers Æthelred and Alfred during his reign, as he had said he would. But when he died in 865 power passed to the eldest brother in the younger generation of the sons of Æthelwulf. The time had come for Æthelred (865–871) to rule over Wessex. Four brothers had now ruled in one kingdom, and the young Alfred was next in line for the throne. The two younger sons of Æthelwulf were about to step onto the stage of their country's greatest ever drama and face the sons of Ragnar.

Campaign Chronicle

⟢⊶⊷⟣

*Nine years without a break he battled with the
enemy. Sometimes they deceived him with an
uncertain truce. Sometimes he took vengeance on
the deceivers. At length he was reduced to such
straits that, with scarcely three counties,
Hampshire, Wiltshire and Somerset, remaining
stubbornly in their allegiance, he was actually
forced to take refuge in an island called Athelney,
which from its marshy situation was hardly
accessible. Years afterwards, when happier times
returned, he himself would tell his friends in
cheerful intimacy the story of his adventures and
how he had survived them by the merits of St
Cuthbert – so common is it among mortal men to
recall with pleasure experiences that were fearful at
the time.*

William of Malmesbury

865 The Great Army Arrives in England

The Ravaging of Kent

As men worked near the coast on the fertile fields of the
Kentish countryside, they saw something through the autumn
haze that shocked them: sail after sail, stretching across the
sea – a vision as wide as it was deep. Nothing quite like it had
been seen before, but those Kentish men knew what it was.

865 The Great Army Arrives in England

There had been raiding in Kent in the previous year. That fleet had exacted promises of money but had set about plundering the countryside with impunity against the agreement they had made. But now, 300–400 ships, carrying up to 5,000 people, began to infest the Isle of Thanet yet again.

Those who could remember – or who had heard tell – of the great fleet of 851, which had stormed Canterbury and which had been finally caught and defeated by King Æthelwulf and his son Æthelbald at Aclea in Surrey, will have known to expect grim times. Some will have remembered the stories of the sacking of Winchester just five years earlier. But the present fleet was huge, like an entire nation on the move, reminding men of the days of the great wanderings of folk across Europe centuries before, when their own Saxon ancestors had poured into the east of Britannia to change the cultural complexion of the island forever. And now it was happening again. Long ago it had been Hengist and Horsa at the head of a pagan warband, carving their destiny in a Christian land. Now Halfdan, Ubba and Ivarr – the sons of Ragnar – had come to see what they could snatch.

But despite the ravaging, it soon became clear that neither Kent, nor indeed Thanet, were the target. Instead, this Great Heathen Army sailed away. To East Anglia they went, to the land of King Edmund. The East Anglian king, whose place in English history would be confirmed in the most horrible of ways, had reigned over his people many years and was well loved. Edmund's scouts must have reported what they saw off the East Anglian coast with some trepidation. Nobody knows what Ivarr said to Edmund when they met, but it was likely to have been a one-sided conversation. It must have been very clear to Edmund and his court that the Danes were here to stay. There would be no sporadic raiding, no random devastation. The sons of Ragnar had a different agenda, their ambition driven by cold reason. Money, food, accommodation and horses: these were the bare requirements of the Great Heathen Army.

Edmund was not in a strong enough position to do much about it. The numbers ranged against him were already large and the Danes had pulled off a complete surprise. The news grew worse for the king. Those Vikings who had been active in Francia, and elsewhere on the Continent, had got wind of Ivarr's foothold in East Anglia and joined him in the spring and summer of 866. The brothers had spent a whole winter in England and as the fields of East Anglia became infested with Viking tents and equipment, Edmund must have wondered how to rid himself of the menace. Recently in Francia, Charles the Bald's policy of appeasement had made many in Ivarr's army very rich in terms of portable wealth. They brought to the East Anglian camp large amounts of wine and their share of the 4,000 pounds of silver Charles is known to have paid them. Increasing that wealth was certainly a motivation for the Danes, but the leadership had a political goal, unlike any previous Viking foray on English soil.

The Horsing of the Danes

Asser's statement that 'almost the whole army' was supplied with horses when in East Anglia may reveal a multitude of things. First, it shows that East Anglia was a good breeding ground for horses and presumably held many royal and ecclesiastical studs. Second, it shows the Danes had a military plan. They would campaign on land – many hundreds, if not thousands of them – as a mounted infantry force. Soon the *Anglo-Saxon Chronicle* would refer to them as 'radhere', literally meaning a 'mounted army'. From the sea, the Danes would support their land counterparts and often sail into the places the mounted forces had secured for them. To modern eyes, the Danish land force from East Anglia, when it was on the move, would have taken on the look of a cavalry army, only preferring to dismount and fight shield to shield as infantrymen when it came to an encounter. Their opponents, the Anglo-Saxons, whose nobility are known to have widely used horses, would have to adopt new strategies to capture this force in the English landscape.

The appearance of a huge mounted army at this time in England may well have acted as a catalyst for the Anglo-Saxons' horse management techniques. Before the end of the century specific logistical roles were given to the king's horse thegns, who, like their Carolingian counterparts, were responsible for provisioning the army. It is worth, at this early stage, considering just what kind of logistics would have been involved for both the Danish and Anglo-Saxon mounted forces. Just one horse consumes up to 12 pounds of grain a day and up to 13 pounds of hay. When on campaign, it is likely these mounts were given safe grazing areas. Here, they will have consumed grass amounting to three times the total of hay. This

The Breeding of Horses

The Anglo-Saxons loved their horses. As early as the eighth century the Venerable Bede mentioned the gift by King Oswine (644–651) of a 'royal' horse to St Aidan. That such a horse could have been given as a gift points to the existence of stud farms. The business of running a stud so expertly carried out by monastic communities as well as by king's officials was fraught with difficulty. To breed a horse which was to be involved in warfare was a tricky business. Segregating the mares and ensuring the appropriate stallions covered the right mares was also difficult. The Great Heathen Army which landed in East Anglia in its urgency to provide mounts for itself will have destroyed generations of horse breeding across the kingdom. Just one hole in a fence could destroy a breeding programme, let alone an army of marauding Danes.

In Alfredian times a charter of the puppet king Ceolwulf (874–*c*. 880) dating to 875 gives us a clue as to contemporary horse management. Ceolwulf freed 'the whole diocese of the Hwicce from feeding the king's horses and those who lead them'. The *Anglo-Saxon Chronicle* records the English army as often riding after the Danes and in many cases catching up with them. The Danes themselves valued their horses and are even known to have captured them in one country and shipped them to another, the case of Rochester in 885 being a good example.

is notwithstanding the many gallons of water required for each animal each day. And so, as they destroyed numerous studs across the ancient kingdom of East Anglia and prepared for a lengthy campaign, the Danes cannot have known that they were changing the way warfare would be waged in England for years to come.

866 Descent on York

All Saints Day, 1 November 866

King Burgred of Mercia had come to his throne in 852. Although he headed a family at loggerheads with other Mercian clans, all vying for the throne, Burgred enjoyed a relatively civil relationship with Wessex. He had appealed to Alfred's father for help in Mercia's long-standing struggle against the Welsh and Æthelwulf had indeed answered his call. But the time for testing the strength of the marriage of Alfred's sister to the Mercian king was yet to come.

As it grew in the countryside of East Anglia and provisioned itself, the sheer size of the Great Heathen Army must have terrified those Mercian scouts who rode from Burgred's kingdom. Which way would it go when the campaigning season started? Burgred, whose military capabilities had already been proved to some extent against the Welsh, knew that this new threat was different. If they came directly for him, could he resist? Was there even enough unity within his court to prevent this colossal enemy from driving apart the nobility of ancient Mercia?

Burgred had every reason to be afraid, but if he had kept a close eye on the build-up of the Danes, then the same could not have been said for the leadership of Northumbria. In fact, this most ancient and one time leading Anglo-Saxon kingdom, had descended into political farce on the eve of the Viking invasion, and it is certainly not beyond the intelligence apparatus available to Ivarr for him to have known almost every detail about the situation in what would now become the first of many strategic targets.

Asser bemoans the situation in the north as having been

'fomented by the devil'. The Northumbrians, he tells us, had expelled their king Osberht, replacing him with a tyrant called Ælle, a man not of the royal line. This sort of diversion from the royal bloodline was always a contentious issue in Anglo-Saxon society. The alleged usurpation had occurred in 858. Nor did Ælle rule without the prospect of the return of Osberht, who was still at large. It had been Ælle who, according to legend, had killed Ragnar, and it would be he who would pay dearly for it. His war with Osberht reduced the Northumbrian country-side to poverty, particularly in respect of the robbing of the lands of the community of Lindisfarne. Some legends say that Osberht had raped the wife of a man called Bruern Brocard, and that Brocard was so set on revenge that he sailed to Denmark and enlisted the aid of the sons of Ragnar. Whatever the truth behind the story, the leading thegns of the Northumbrian kingdom were divided in their loyalties: on the one side, to a strong-willed and popular incumbent, and on the other, to the one-time occupant of the throne who was entitled to the position by virtue of his blood. What happened next in Northumbria might seem like a tale of vengeance, where saga and reality briefly came together in a colourful northern world.

But summer turned into autumn and still the Danes had not moved. If Burgred's scouts were surprised at the immobility of a force seemingly ready for campaign and yet going nowhere, then, to the feuding northerners, such news – if it was ever received – might have vindicated their disregard for the danger. Ælle and Osberht should have realised they were mistaken. These two Anglo-Saxon leaders were scorned by the Scandinavian writers and poets of the age. They were the 'pigs' who would soon 'grunt', so the legend had said.

And the Danish leadership was clever in its approach. Ivarr, whose legendary father had apparently adopted such a strat-agem in an Easter time attack on Paris, knew the value of timing. His enemy, after a year of campaigning in its own kingdom against its own kind, would be exhausted by winter. They would also be thinking of other things.

Quite how many thousands went with the brothers to York that winter, and how many were left behind to garrison themselves at their camp in East Anglia, we will never know. We can only guess at the mixture of relief and awe the Mercians felt when they heard that the force was sailing north, over the mouth of the Humber. The Danes had chosen to head not for Burgred's Mercia but for the crippled and divided patrimony of Ælle.

On Friday, 1 November 866, they came. It was All Saints Day, an important religious festival in the Northumbrian calendar. This was an ideal time to attack, just when folk were putting aside their weapons and turning to matters of faith. The sanctity of the day meant nothing to Ivarr, just as it had meant nothing to Ragnar that day long ago in Paris. If it meant anything, it represented a golden opportunity.

The surprise was total. In fact, Ivarr was almost too successful in his assault on York. Both claimants to the throne were there that day, and they both fled the city in the rout, leaving behind annihilated supporters on both sides. As the Great Heathen Army moved into York, Ivarr must have been delighted with his prize. The jewel of the north, a great trading centre with contacts all over the known world, this ancient city, so beloved by Roman emperors, would become the pride of the Scandinavian north for at least a century. But as he settled his forces in the city for the winter, he knew there was work to do. Preparations must be made. What if the two escapees were to return united with a combined force to push him out of his new possession? It would be a cold and uneasy winter in York for the sons of Ragnar, but it was colder still for the men who, for the time being, had been banished to the barren countryside.

867 An English Disaster

Palm Sunday, 23 March 867

Somehow, against the expectations of many, the two protagonists in Northumbria's protracted succession crisis called a halt to their war. We cannot know what was said between them, but over those winter months, and into the spring, preparations were made by both parties to launch an assault on occupied York. They would do to Ivarr what he had done to them. Ivarr, if he had indeed been busy preparing York for what was to come, had not done so by repairing the old Roman walls, which still had many gaps in them.

Osberht and Ælle chose Palm Sunday – a major feast day – to attack. Perhaps they had learned from the disaster of 1 November the previous year, or perhaps they thought Ivarr simply would not expect such tactics to be employed on a Christian city by its former Christian rulers. From what we can gather, the first attack successfully pushed those Danes formed up outside the city to the rear. It might have seemed to the allies for a moment that the tables had been turned on their enemy and that surprise had once again won the day. But Osberht and Ælle were forcing their way into a hornet's nest. Through the broken walls they pushed a retreating enemy into the crowded streets, where thousands of Danes had drawn their swords and readied their spears. It was carnage. Whether it was a ruse to draw the enemy in, or whether it was just their good fortune that they were able to swamp the enemy army in the narrow streets, we cannot tell. Asser says that the defenders were driven on by grief and necessity and so attacked fiercely. This much notwithstanding, the result was a catastrophic defeat for Ælle and Osberht. Along with eight leading Northumbrian ealdormen, the two kings paid with their own lives for the revenge attack on the Danes. The transition of this great northern jewel from the Anglian settlement of Eoforwic to the Viking city of Jorvik had begun. Both inside and outside the town the Danes overthrew their adversaries and those few who survived on the attacking side were forced to make peace with Ivarr. The pigs had grunted.

According to legend, and especially the *Tale of the Sons of Ragnar*, Ælle did not die immediately. He was brought to Ivarr and the brutal pagan rite of the blood eagle was performed upon him in front of a bloodthirsty audience: his chest ripped open and the lungs ripped out and displayed on his back in the mark of the eagle. And all of this in praise to Odin for the victory. Did it happen? Can the sagas and the reality be reconciled with one another? Perhaps we should hold onto this one thought for now: the ninth century, as we shall see from the relationships which unfold below, was an age where seemingly far-fetched stories of political revenge were almost indistinguishable from reality. It was a dangerous and treacherous world for anyone of importance.

Consolidation and Opportunity

Despite a comprehensive victory, and the removal of Ælle and Osberht, Ivarr decided not to rule Northumbria from his seat in York. The canny Dane knew very well that ancient Northumbria was built on familial ties of kinship, so he installed a puppet king called Ecgberht. Ecgberht is a figure of uncertain background to us, but it is likely he was carefully chosen to suit the politics of the kingdom. The agreement – if later Danish agreements with their English puppets are anything to go by – would have run along the lines of Ecgberht having to keep the kingdom open for the return of the main part of the Great Heathen Army when its leaders had decided they had had enough of campaigning and wished to settle the land and rule it.

Further south, those Mercian scouts would have brought word to Burgred of Ælle's death (whichever way it came about) and the news must have crippled him. The threat to his kingdom had not passed after all. Now it was stronger than before, as the Danes sat in a menacing position at the heart of Northumbria, turning what had been a conveniently fragmented nation into a new military threat. If he had known where they were headed that winter, his heart would have quickened. Ivarr had chosen to head directly south by land and took his force to Nottingham. Nottingham would become, in the next generation, a major Danish stronghold, and it is easy to see why. It commands a central position in the northern district of Mercia and has a navigable river running through it. From here, if he could establish himself safely and quickly enough in Asser's 'city of caves', Ivarr could dictate his demands to the Mercians.

868 A Plea to Wessex

Nottingham

The value of an alliance between Mercia and Wessex must have seemed greater than ever now. Æthelred of Wessex, already married to Wulfthryth, and with two small children, could hardly be approached to form a traditional marriage alliance with Mercia, but Alfred, now, according to Asser, the 'heir apparent' in Wessex, was without a wife. And so, with Burgred's blessing (for it was Burgred who was married to Alfred's sister) the nineteen-year-old West Saxon ætheling was married, some time in 868, to Ealhswith, daughter of another Æthelred 'Mucil', of a now forgotten Mercian noble tribe called the Gaini. Ealhswith's mother was herself of the royal Mercian line and her noble bearing attracted a nod of approval from Asser himself.

Burgred was right to look south for help. He had feared this turn of events for some time. The Danes had a power base in York, sure enough, but its recent ravaging through years of warfare had turned that country into a wasteland. Certainly, for the Danes, there was the trade generated by the city to take account of, but that was not instant wealth. It would take time to build upon existing networks. What Ivarr and his kin wanted was more wealth and greater power. So they looked to the rich lands of Mercia.

Ivarr got what he wanted. He had arrived at Nottingham in full force before Burgred could guess where he would strike and before the Mercian king could summon his fyrd. Burgred had immediately sent word south on hearing the news. The strength of the growing alliance between Wessex and Mercia must be tested. From Æthelred he requested urgent military aid. Perhaps the Great Heathen Army could be defeated by the combined fyrds of the two kingdoms, now that they had the enemy in one place.

Help from the two brothers was apparently easily obtained, for Asser states that they 'promptly fulfilled their promise'. Thus, from every corner of Wessex, an army was summoned. When ready, this force headed north into Mercia to meet, for the first time, the full might of what would become its most bitter enemy.

But Anglo-Saxon fyrds took time to raise. As Burgred watched the Danes ensconce themselves behind their own fortifications at Nottingham, as he saw the smoke rising from the makeshift hearths and heard the sounds of thousands of foreign voices taunting him, he must have hoped for good news from the south. On the Continent, the Danes had shown they had no stomach for sieges. Burgred will have known of the calamities that had befallen besieged Danes in Francia, and must have wanted to repeat them at Nottingham.

Eventually, the West Saxon brothers did indeed turn up with their armies, but what they saw must have deflated their spirits. They had wanted to give battle: the Danes preferred to sit it out in their stronghold. The *Anglo-Saxon Chronicle* says that 'no heavy fighting occurred there' and Asser reports that the Christians were 'unable to breach the wall'. It seems that some limited attempt to test the defences of this giant encampment was made by the Anglo-Saxons, but to no avail. Nor were they apparently able to exact a proper stranglehold on the enemy position, since there is no indication that the Danes were unable to support themselves during the siege.

It was a humiliation. Ivarr had come to test them and the Anglo-Saxons had been found wanting. They could not get at his army, could not starve it out. Ivarr knew that if the Mercian king wanted him to leave Nottingham, he would have to come to terms, would have to offer him something. It was the politics of intimidation, and it worked time and again for the Danes, across Christendom and beyond. Where battle could be avoided, it was avoided, and still the prizes would come. We are told the Mercians 'made peace' with the Heathen Army and that the brothers went back to Wessex without any real fighting having taken place. We must assume that Mercian coffers were emptied of tribute, but just how much silver was being taken from Burgred at Nottingham, and just how much he had left, we cannot know.

As the brothers turned south, Alfred's mind must have been on his forthcoming wedding, which took place at the royal vill of Sutton Courtenay in Berkshire. A great gathering it would have been too. But the nobility of Wessex were worried. The heir apparent had been part of a great climb-down at Nottingham, in the face of a potentially fatal threat to the country. Furthermore, as Alfred doubled up in pain, clutching his stomach in front of the assembled wedding guests, people must have wondered if he could cope with what seemed like a permanent illness, as well as the pressures of military campaigning. These were anxious times for the Anglo-Saxons.

869 The Danes on the Move

The Calling of York

Whatever the deal at Nottingham, the chronicles record that the Danes left the place on horseback and returned to York, where they remained for one year. Throughout the greater part of 869, they made sure of their northern conquest. Their puppet, Ecgberht, was quizzed as to how he was holding the country open for Ivarr, and how he was suppressing any signs of rebellion among other claimant families to the ancient throne. Wulfhere, the archbishop of York – who had not, in fact, suffered enforced conversion to paganism or anything like it – will have had many audiences with the Danish leadership over that long year in the northern capital. It certainly seemed that the Danish hold on York was strong. People came to the newly established puppet king from all over the country during the summer and autumn of 869, and with Ivarr standing at his shoulder, a multitude of deals were brokered with disaffected nobility across the whole of England.

The Ride to Thetford

Mercia held its breath. The tribute paid to the Danes at Nottingham and the promises presumably extracted from them not to attack would mean nothing if the giant army that set out from York in the autumn of 869 headed for the centre of Burgred's kingdom. He would be undone. Part of the Nottingham agreement may have been designed to prevent such an occurrence at someone else's expense. For when the

The Viking Wars of Alfred the Great

Danes pressed south along the Roman road of Ermine Street, they headed not for the Mercian heartland, but for East Anglia, via Peterborough. No hint of treachery, no hint of broken promises. Ivarr was travelling through the eastern reaches of Burgred's kingdom with a different destination in mind.

The monasteries of the east were plundered. Peterborough suffered awfully. This famous community, whose scribes would later play a part in recording these dreadful days of English history, was ruthlessly sacked by the pagans. The abbot and many of his monks were slain. The rape of Peterborough was such that a local scribe claimed the Danes 'had brought it about so that what was earlier very rich was as it were nothing'. Meanwhile, the local *Crowland Chronicle* states that, during these attacks, just one boy, 'fair in form and face', survived the onslaught and was taken by the Danes as a pet, but later managed to escape. No one knows who the boy was or where he went, but more importantly, a later and valuable chronicle by John of Peterborough tells us who was responsible for this shocking devastation and carnage: it was Ubba, Ivarr's brother.

The East Anglian campaign of 869 is shrouded in legend. Not, as it happens, shrouded in Scandinavian legend for once, but in the legend of the man who paid for defeat with his life. In a perverse way, it was the Danes' first political mistake in England. We owe much of our knowledge of this to Abbo of Fleury, who travelled to England in the tenth century to pick up the pieces of the tale, but what he tells has a ring of truth about it. Abbo, on his trip to England, had interviewed an archbishop who had known King Edmund's armour bearer. From this man a story was reconstructed. Ivarr had descended on Edmund's kingdom 'like a wolf'. Edmund had been taken by surprise. Perhaps Edmund's agreement with Ivarr had precluded such an attack. Perhaps – as is suggested elsewhere – Ubba had come by sea in an effort to split the responding forces of the East Anglian king, who would then literally have been caught between the devil and the deep blue sea. However they came, the game was up for Edmund. The pagans would stay over the winter in the heart of the kingdom, which had previously accommodated them. They chose Thetford to set their camp.

869 The Danes on the Move

This town, where the Little Ouse crosses the Icknield Way, was strategically well placed to allow the Danes a number of options when deciding their next move. To the south lay London and Wessex, and to the west lay Mercia. But for the moment, there was business to be done in East Anglia.

A Cult is Born, 26 November 869

Ivarr sent a message to Edmund. It must have been similar in character to the directive given to Ecgberht of Northumbria. Ivarr clearly wanted Edmund to behave as a puppet. His messenger, according to the flowery language of Abbo, delivered the following statement to the East Anglian king at his hall in Hellesdon, Norfolk, saying:

> Ivarr, our king, bold and victorious on sea and on land, has dominion over many peoples, and has now come to this country with his army to take up winter-quarters with his men. He commands that you share your hidden gold-hordes and your ancestral possessions with him straight away, and that you become his vassal-king, if you want to stay alive, since you now don't have the forces that you can resist him.

These famous words may or may not have been spoken. However, the response was predictable: the king would have none of it. Edmund may have felt he had no immediate ability to meet the military threat; may have gambled on stalling the Dane while forces could be raised; he may even have thought he already had men enough. But to refuse the advances of a triumphant Viking leader was to sign your own death warrant. Edmund is supposed to have replied that he would submit only if Ivarr became Christian. Soon, the renowned East Anglian king would be dragged from his hall to pay a heavy price for his demands. What followed, on 26 November 869, may have been a battle between the Great Heathen Army and such forces as were at Edmund's side, or it might have been a summary execution. Asser has it as a battle, in which many were lost on the English side. Either way, Edmund was killed and in an instant transported from a slot in Anglo-Saxon history to a slot in eternity, as one of England's most celebrated saints. The brutality of the legends that have him tortured, beaten and used as archery practice is matched by the lingering, melancholic magic of the Christian memory. The head, which was cruelly severed and discarded, would speak to those who came to look for it in the woods, guiding them towards it. Here was a hagiographer's dream. The community at Bury St Edmunds became one of the great power houses of the medieval monastic movement in the centuries that followed, but most importantly, for the time being, the Danes realised they had made a mistake. Within a single generation, Danish leaders of the north would be minting coins in celebration of Edmund, a saint created by the cruel hands of their own kinsmen. The dispatching of Edmund marked a turning point in the way the Scandinavians dealt with their leading political opponents. Summary violence by way of execution would not necessarily bring the dividends desired.

That said, the appearance in East Anglia at this time of a mysterious new coinage, minted in the names of two Englishmen, Æthelred and Oswald, might indicate that Ivarr did at least manage to establish client rulers in East Anglia. But the fact that the Great Heathen Army was once again encamped in the eastern kingdom was testimony enough to who held the real power.

Here, however, we arrive at our first big problem in piecing together what really happened in 869–870. The chronicler Æthelweard, who is usually reliable – or at the very least tantalising in his unique revelations – tells us that Ivarr died the same year Edmund was slain. And yet a scan of wider sources reveals something quite different and all the more fascinating. For the first time, it seems that the Great Heathen Army split. Ivarr appears in the Irish annals for the year 870, energetically campaigning around Dumbarton, alongside Olaf of the Dublin Vikings, with the Picts being the unfortunate sufferers. Ivarr's campaigns in the north mark the origin of what would become a thorn in the side of tenth-century southern English kings. The creation of a Scandinavian power block straddling northern

870 Assault on Wessex

Britain and Ireland, from York to Dublin, with a friendly or subservient Dumbarton at the centre in Strathclyde, would preoccupy the mind of King Athelstan (924–939), Alfred's grandson, and ultimately lead to one of the greatest showdowns ever seen on British soil. But for now, here in the winter of 869, there sat in East Anglia a still sizeable army under Halfdan, another son of Ragnar, pondering its next move. With Ivarr gone, and a new campaign about to unfold, the chronicles begin to reveal some new names to add to the old. What their fate would be and where their targets lay, a brief span of time would tell.

Whether it was as a result of the Nottingham agreement, or simply sheer luck, Burgred must have breathed a sigh of relief when he heard where they were going. Halfdan, and a new leader named Bagsecg, had struck out, not for Mercia, but for the kingdom they knew had riches as yet untapped and a relatively untried king. The Danes had chosen Æthelred I's Wessex. For the king and his teenage brother, the time had come.

870 Assault on Wessex

Reading

It was not until the autumn of 870 that people knew the Great Heathen Army's exact intentions. The Danish army of 'hateful memory' then left East Anglia and marched directly for the royal estate at Reading, in Berkshire, its plan to occupy a place on the strategic communications network, in a commanding and intimidating position above Wessex, in much the same way it had chosen the Mercian town of Nottingham. A naval contingent also sailed up the Thames to Reading. The fact that Reading was a royal estate, in a land rich in resources and nearby monastic wealth, must also have been taken into account.

Berkshire had not long been under the wing of the kings of Wessex. Only since the 850s had the government and ownership of this area been handed to the kingdom south of the river. But by choosing to descend upon a royal estate, the Danes were satisfying two military needs in terms of both practicality and the element of surprise. Reading will have been stuffed with the annual food rents, presided over at such places by a king's reeve. These rents will have been delivered largely on the hoof and in bundles of supplies for the winter. The time had not yet come in Anglo-Saxon history when the obligation to deliver such tax had been commuted to cash payments. Just as importantly, the taking of such a place would have denied its resources to Æthelred. So take it they did, and as an additional assurance of their own safety, they fortified their new position strongly.

The Battle of Englefield, Sunday, 31 December 870

South of the estate at Reading, the rivers Thames and Kennet converge. Using these two rivers as two sides of a defensive triangle, the Danes erected an earthwork to provide protection on a third side, which they punctuated with a number of gates, and in all probability added a timber palisade as well. They were effectively hemming themselves in. Local historians identify the Plummery Ditch, still a water-filled dyke in 1816, as the defensive work stretching from one river to the other. If this is so, at around 800 yards long, it was one side of a triangle that could have housed upwards of 1,000 people.

Safe in the knowledge that no Christian king would surely attack them during the twelve days of Christmas, the Danes set about their engineering works and were even bold enough to send out a large detachment for the purposes of routine plunder. But the two jarls who confidently marched across the Berkshire countryside were about to be confounded. Not everyone had turned their back on the dangers posed by the Danes of Reading that Christmas.

Just three days after their arrival at Reading, and while their kin were working on their new fortification, Jarl Sidroc marched his Danish detachment around the north of the great Windsor forest and clung to the banks of the Kennet, soon finding the area known locally as 'the plain of the Angles' or Englefield. He was 10 miles to the west of Reading. With the camp at Reading so far behind him, his heart must have sunk when the small retinue of Æthelwulf, the ealdorman of Berkshire, who had already established himself in 860 when he surprised Weland after the burning of Winchester, tore into the enemy on an icy field on New Year's Eve. Æthelwulf was making a name for himself as a strategically gifted commander.

The battle was hard fought, as chroniclers often tell us they are, but so effective was Æthelwulf's ambush, it accounted for Jarl Sidroc and another leading jarl. News of the losses would be difficult to bear for the main Danish force back at Reading. As the routed stragglers fell back from Englefield upon their line of march and returned in disarray to the camp, the nature of the calamity dawned on Bagsecg and Halfdan. Nothing quite like this had happened to them before. It was only a small defeat, but had they stumbled into the wrong kingdom? Was it not the kingdom of Wessex, under another Æthelwulf, which, in the 850s, had repeatedly rebuffed their kinsmen in previous campaigns? Two of Halfdan's jarls had just been eliminated in an unambiguous defeat at the hands of a supposedly cowering enemy. Danish hands quickened their work on the ditch and palisade at Reading.

Æthelwulf's retinue, which had pulled off its masterpiece at Englefield, cannot have been large. He could not, for example, have been expected to blockade the Danes at the camp. So the riders who hurried south to bring welcome news to the royal brothers of Wessex, came also with a plea for aid. Immediately on hearing it, Æthelred and Alfred, with their combined forces, quickly made for Reading. They must already have been at arms, since it took just four days for them to arrive, fully equipped for war, outside the gates of the Danish camp.

871 Ashdown and the Year of the Great Battles

And that year there were nine national fights fought against the raiding army in the kingdom south of the Thames, besides those forays which Alfred the king's brother, and single ealdorman and king's thegns often rode on, which were never counted.

Anglo-Saxon Chronicle,
Winchester Manuscript (A), 871

The Viking Wars of Alfred the Great

The Siege at Reading, 3 January 871

When the English armies arrived at the camp, they found a number of unsuspecting Danes outside the gates of their newly built fortification. Quickly and unceremoniously these people were cut down. But at that point a storm of warriors poured from the gates of the camp, set out for this very purpose, and with such ferocity that they enjoyed an emphatic victory. Asser, who normally does not appear impressed with the heathen fighters, says:

> Like wolves they burst out of all the gates and joined battle with all their might [. . .] the Christians eventually turned their backs and the Vikings won the victory and were masters of the battlefield.

But what Asser does not say is how utterly routed the armies of the two West Saxon brothers truly were. They had been swamped by an army they should have been besieging. It was even worse than Nottingham. The twelfth-century chronicler, Gaimar, is clearer than Asser on the matter, and must have had his hands on a now long-lost but valuable historical manuscript:

> The fourth day after king Æthelred
> Came and his brother Ælfred,
> To Reading, with a great host,
> And the Danes soon sallied out.
> In an open field they fought a battle
> Which did not cease all day.
> There was Æthelwulf slain,
> The great man of whom I just spoke,
> And Æthelred and Ælfred
> Were driven to Wiscelet [Whistley].
> This is a ford towards Windsor,
> Near a lake in a marsh.
> Thither the one host came pursuing,
> And did not know the ford over the river [Loddon].

871 Ashdown and the Year of the Great Battles

Twyford has ever been the name of the ford,
At which the Danes turned back,
And the English escaped.

If the embarrassment was not enough for Æthelred and Alfred, when their men were finally able to return to the battlefield to assume the grim task of identifying the fallen, while feeling the smirking gaze of Danish faces at their backs, they brought back to the royal brothers further bad news. The hero of Englefield was dead. Æthelweard, in his account of the battle, reveals a curious fact about the late Æthelwulf of Berkshire, master of the art of the ambush: he was a Mercian and not a West Saxon. Not only this, Æthelweard says:

> In fact, the body of the Dux mentioned above was carried away secretly and taken into Mercia to the place called Northworthig, but 'Derby' in the Danish tongue.

It was some journey for the dead man. Nominally under West Saxon control, Berkshire had retained its Mercian ealdorman until the very day he died defending Wessex. Æthelweard's statement shows that the recent alliance between Wessex and Mercia was still one of convenience. There would need to be a sea change in the relations between the two kingdoms to remove the divide. But it also reveals that by the tenth century, the time when Æthelweard was writing, the place names of the north Midlands were changing, and in this particular case the Danish 'Derby' has for ten centuries won the argument over the English 'Northworthy', which has disappeared beneath the Viking waves.

The Danes were delighted with their victory. Englefield was but a bad memory for them, even though it happened just days earlier. It was time now for the Danes to exploit this astounding success, to push into the countryside and seek a result against Wessex. If Wessex should fall now, if the last two adult descendants of King Ecgberht could be eliminated, then only Mercia lay in the way of a new Danish order being established, which would stretch from the border with Cornwall to the

Viking Tactics

Two basic formations appear to have been in operation in the Viking armies. First, there was the shield-wall, or *skaldborg*. The shield wall gave protection along the line with each man in the unit overlapping his shield with his neighbour. Breaches in the wall were often exploited by the enemy. These units were often several ranks deep with only the front adopting the shield wall formation. There are hints from some very late sources that the Vikings might even have been able to adopt a circular formation with the front rank displaying interlocking shields.

A more offensive formation was the swine-array or *Svinfylka*. Attributed to the god Odin himself, this was an infantry wedge-shaped formation which in reality seems to have been 'borrowed' from the late Roman period training manual. If we are to believe the later Icelandic sagas, the swine-array consisted of a front rank containing two warriors and a second rank of three, a third of four, and so forth. These men, armed with javelins, spears and double-edged swords, would crash into enemy lines having first hurled their missiles and then drawn their swords at the point of impact. Their intent was to smash their way into the enemy shield wall and break it, carving a gap which those behind them and to the sides of the triangle could exploit. These swine arrays may only have numbered just twelve men, but their ferocity frequently proved unbearable.

border with Scotland. And Halfdan knew it. The stage was set for the first major set piece battle between the kingdom of Wessex and the Great Heathen Army. Enter the wild boar of Ashdown ridge.

The Battle of Ashdown, 8 January 871

Just four days after their defeat, the brothers managed to rally their men. The king knew that if Halfdan and Bagsecg were to

871 Ashdown and the Year of the Great Battles

strike into Wessex, they would need to head west along the Icknield Way. It is probable that Halfdan had either Wallingford or Abingdon in his sights: if so, the king must stop them. The brave Æthelwulf of Berkshire may well have been engaged at Englefield in denying the Danes a reconnaissance opportunity to this effect. And so, upon Kingstanding Hill, west of a ford across the Thames at Moulsford, at a place known as Ashdown, Æthelred set his camp, straddling the ancient Roman road. It was the morning of 8 January.

Sure enough, the enemy came. When the Danes saw the English throng beneath them as they climbed the crest of the hill, they knew that battle would surely follow. They would not necessarily have relished it, but for the leadership, the stakes were too high to be picky about irreplaceable losses. Face it they must. They were, after all, experienced warriors with, until recently, an impeccable track record on campaign.

As the young Alfred gazed across the valley he noticed something unusual happening, something impressive. The Danes were dividing their forces for deployment. The Great Heathen Army had arrayed itself in deference to rank. The traditional interpretation of Asser's account is that one division formed up under the two Danish 'kings' Halfdan and Bagsecg, and that the other was commanded by a group of leading Danish jarls. The English response was to form two commands (which it is probable they would have done anyway), one under King Æthelred and the other under Alfred. The idea was that the king's division should be set against that of the Danish kings and Alfred's against the jarls.

But Alfred was ready before his brother. He had been watching the evolutions made by his opposite division across the valley and he knew that if he was not to be cut off by the opposing jarls, then he must strike at them before they drove a wedge between him and his brother and the nearby river. With the shield walls of the Danish divisions already in place above him, Alfred is said to have arrived on the battlefield sooner and in better order than his royal brother. This was due, apparently, to the king's insistence on hearing mass in his tent before engaging the enemy. The Danish phalanx began its customary intimidation, screaming threats and preparing for action. They were in a good position above the English as Alfred advanced up the slope; and with Æthelred seemingly unprepared, they would surely advance and swamp Alfred before he received help: unless, of course, Alfred could do something about it. But Alfred was already demonstrating what is celebrated as his first unilateral command decision. He had decisively chosen to go on the offensive. Asser says he

> could not oppose the enemy battle lines any longer without either retreating from the battlefield or attacking the enemy before his brother's arrival on the scene. He finally deployed the Christian forces against the hostile armies as he had previously intended (even though the king had not yet come), and acting courageously, like a wild boar, supported by divine counsel and strengthened by divine help, when he had closed up the shield wall in proper order, he moved his army without delay against the enemy.

It was all or nothing for Asser's 'heir-apparent'. His brother would surely join him soon, if Alfred could just hold the descending Danes. There is a hint in the passage from Asser that Alfred may have positioned himself at a point where he could, with his own division, make contact with enough frontage to pin both 'hostile armies' in a holding position to prevent them gathering momentum and swamping Æthelred. If so, this was a bold and brave move. Alfred raced up the hill, and with a smaller force, confronted the most fearsome enemy to have fought on English soil for hundreds of years. But for Alfred, if not the Danes, the stakes were high indeed. The two royal brothers were the last adults in the line of the House of Æthelwulf – all that remained were the young children of Æthelred. Should the Danes win at Ashdown, Wessex would be wide open for conquest, and all the careful planning and delicate negotiations their father had undertaken surrounding the West Saxon royal inheritance would count for nothing. Wessex would be a thing of memory, its smouldering churches marking the final act in its moral decline.

And so Alfred's men launched themselves up that slope and crashed into the enemy with all their passion and might. The shuddering contact of the opposing phalanxes was made around a small thorn tree, which Asser says he had seen for himself. Here, 'with loud shouting from all', Alfred held and held. Mercifully, into the fray marched Æthelred. Thus, with divine inspiration dutifully invoked, and just about in the nick of time, Æthelred bore down onto what would have been the exposed flank of the Danish kings' division, as it was attempting to envelop and roll up the line of Alfred's smaller holding force. Here, for the first time since they had so easily carved their way through the Anglo-Saxon kingdoms of England, the Danes found themselves in a traditional large-scale infantry engagement, where defeat would be decided by the side that broke first. It was not the preferred Viking method of war, but it was meat and drink for the Anglo-Saxons.

The Danes broke first. The Jarls' division had clearly struggled to withstand Alfred's action against them. They had fought for a long time and five of their leaders had been killed in the action. If the leaderless remainder of that division was preparing to withdraw, their despair would have turned to panic when they learned that the banner of Bagsecg had fallen just yards away. The day was lost, and every man must now flee, attempting only to save himself. Even in blind panic the natural tendency of a shattered army is to fall back on its line of march, to where it knows there is both supply and safety. And so, as a wintry darkness descended over Ashdown, the fleeing Danes scampered, bloodied and exhausted, back to their Reading encampment, where the sight that met those who had remained was one of shock and surprise.

But the brothers had not finished with the Danes. When set piece battles occurred in Anglo-Saxon England, as opposed to the types of encounter we have so far observed, there was always a great carnage during the rout. Sometimes we hear the chroniclers talk of the winning side having 'mastery of the battlefield', but here, at Ashdown, we are told the English pursued the Danes from the battlefield until nightfall. This may well have been an action carried out by mounted troops in reserve, hacking at the heels of an exhausted enemy. The defeated refugees of the battle of Ashdown left behind them the bodies of many of their leaders, scattered over all parts of the battlefield. Amid this gory scene of carnage lay King Bagsecg, Jarl Sidroc the Old, Jarl Sidroc the Younger, Jarl Osbern, Jarl Fræna and Jarl Harold.

Early the following morning, stragglers who had somehow managed to escape the mounted patrols came to the camp at Reading to join the others. When the great wooden gates were closed behind the last of them, Halfdan knew that, with his depleted force too shattered and too nervous to forage in hostile territory, he would surely not be able to survive for long: but what should he do? Whatever plans he had laid, he knew one thing: the West Saxons had the ability to defend themselves.

The Battle of Basing

The journey would be a little longer than the hapless forage to Englefield or the march that led to disaster at Ashdown, but it might just bring things to a head. Halfdan had been obliged to rethink his plans. The new idea, or so it seemed, was that Halfdan should attempt a knockout blow, avoiding, if at all possible, another of those colossal pitched battles where a Danish victory would perhaps do no more for Halfdan than award him a place in history alongside the legendary ancient commander Pyrrhus of Epirus.

And so the gates opened at Reading once again and the newly invigorated Danes spilled out, with the royal vill at Basing their target, just a day's march to the south and packed with winter supplies. The site of the battle of Basing is said to have been 18 miles south of the Reading camp, in Hackwood Park. If they could capture the vill, then Winchester lay to the south. No matter where Alfred and Æthelred were, if Winchester fell, the game was over.

The Anglo-Saxon fyrd girded its loins for its fourth battle within a month. Many of them, fatigued from their efforts in what they would have considered a kingdom-saving victory, were depressed to find the enemy no longer embarrassed or remorseful under the watchful eyes of God. These exhausted men would have to do it all again. Æthelred's men were called into service much the same way they always had been, but nothing quite so demanding of their lordship bonds had been asked of the fyrd before. They were spent. Some may still have been revelling in the glorious – and seemingly terminal – victory of Ashdown, just two weeks earlier. But Halfdan was heading for Basing, and so, too, were the weary forces of Wessex's royal brothers.

And yet there was something different in the encounter that took place at Basing. Two foes, who now knew each other well, had met again, not perhaps to decide the fate of a people, but to see who could push the other out of the way first. No doubt it was a bloody encounter, no doubt it was hard fought, and no doubt the battle lines were formed in the usual way on both sides. But this was no Ashdown. The result was a winning draw for the Danes. They held the battlefield and the Anglo-Saxons were forced to flee and regroup for another exhausting effort some other day, leaving behind their precious winter supplies. But the Danes patrolled the blood-soaked battlefield at Basing with mixed feelings that evening. They, too, were beginning to understand the meaning of exhaustion.

The Battle of Meretun, Thursday, 22 March 871

Some time passed. The Danes had been checked, albeit at great expense to Wessex, and a direct assault on Winchester looked unlikely. In fact, the Anglo-Saxons were probably not in a position to prevent the Danes from striking at Wallingford again, but even if this did happen, Alfred knew the enemy was unlikely to move directly south for the time being.

So, as winter gave way to spring, the young ætheling arranged a meeting. Æthelred and Alfred met at the unidentified site of Swineborg, to settle matters regarding the West Saxon inheritance. As we have seen, since the days of Æthelwulf, the division of estates at the time of the death of a king could give rise to generations of competing factions. And now, with the two brothers – the last adult males in the line of Æthelwulf – facing danger on the battlefield, the time had come to make an agreement. Both knew that either one of them might die in the weeks ahead. They had been responsible for the death of several enemy kings and jarls and must have thought it only a matter of time before God took one or both of them in this great struggle against the heathen. As Alfred later recalled in his will, they agreed at Swinebeorg that

> Whichever of us lived longer should succeed both to lands and treasures and to all the other's possessions except the part of which each of us had bequeathed to his children.

At this time those children would have been very young. Æthelred's two boys, Æthelwold and Æthelhelm, were too young to have personally influenced the arrangement, but as we shall see, one of them was not without some political support as he grew up. It would also seem that Alfred's marriage to Ealhswith had produced their first child, a daughter named Æthelflæd. This girl would go on to become one of Anglo-Saxon England's most celebrated women, commanding her own armies in the Midlands, as she took back Danish stronghold after stronghold in the great campaigns of the early tenth century, fighting sometimes alongside Edward, her royal brother. But here in 871, Edward was as yet unborn. Other matters were pressing now. No sooner had the brothers confirmed their agreement than some long expected news arrived. The Danes had stirred again.

The king and his brother responded quickly. Their men were growing used to rushing for their horses in the cold winter mornings, used also to the sound of mailcoats clanking against shields, to the smell of leather and wool tinged with blood and sweat. Most of all, these fyrdsmen – many of whom had already lost friends at the hands of, what seemed to them, a tireless enemy – were used to the feeling of trepidation in the pit of their stomachs. They were on the march yet again.

The West Saxon army fought its next battle at a place called

871 Ashdown and the Year of the Great Battles

Meretun. The battle was fought on Thursday, 22 March 871, and is the most problematic battle of those great encounters in the year of battles. Its exact location is unknown, although it is likely to have been at Marten, 20 miles north of Wilton. Here, the Inkpen Ridgeway could provide the means for travel for the combined fyrds of Berkshire and Hampshire to rendezvous before facing the enemy. The ideal place for such a gathering would have been the old Iron Age fort at Walbury Camp, a place that would become a well defended refuge again in a few years time. It was situated in the Severnake Gap, between the two forests of Severnake and Windsor, and thus, when occupied by an army, denied access to any enemy coming from the north to the interior of Wessex. In fact, it may have been to this place the Anglo-Saxon army retired after the defeat at Basing. But its exact location is not the only problem thrown up by the enigmatic battle of Meretun. For some reason, Asser completely neglects to mention it. The *Anglo-Saxon Chronicle*, however, presents an account from which we might draw a few tentative conclusions:

> And two months later, King Æthelred and Alfred, his brother, fought against the raiding army at Merton and they were in two bands, and they put both to flight and for long in the day had the victory, and there was great slaughter on either side, and the Danish had possession of the place of slaughter; and Bishop Heahmund [of Sherborne] was killed there and many good men.

A passage capable of a number of interpretations. Here is one: the brothers had faced the enemy who 'were in two bands'. They had been divided thus at Ashdown, but it is not clear here whether we have a repeat of the Ashdown formation, or whether one division at Meretun was that of Halfdan and the other that of some new Danish arrival. The chronicler follows up his account of the battle by saying that only afterwards were the Danes joined by the new army. However, the account of Meretun is unusual and unlike any of the others. Why had the English technically lost a battle which, for so long, they had seemed to be winning? Had there been a deliberate tactical withdrawal or was there another reason? The answer may lie in what happened to the king of Wessex just a month or so later. Æthelred, son of Æthelwulf, departed from the beautiful and brutal world of Anglo-Saxon England at the tender age of twenty-five. Nobody tells us why.

The Battle of Wilton, May 871

If Æthelred had been wounded at the battle of Meretun it might go some way towards explaining the English withdrawal from the field. For Alfred, the wise arrangements made at Swinebeorg were to be realised all too soon. Alfred, the last of the sons of Æthelwulf, was now king of Wessex. As he buried his brother at the spiritual home of West Saxon kings, Alfred walked through the royal mausoleum at Wimborne, cutting a lonely figure. He had inherited great wealth and land, but had he inherited the political allegiance of those who had been bound by lordship ties to his brother and his brother's children?

Æthelweard is the only chronicler to tell us that while the funeral proceedings were taking place, somewhere in the kingdom of Wessex another military engagement with the Danes was being fought. If he was right, we know next to nothing of it, except for what he tells us. It would seem the men of Wessex were engaging the enemy in yet another costly holding action:

> An innumerable summer army [Sumarliði] arrived at Reading and opened hostilities vigorously against the army of the West Saxons. And the ones who had long been ravaging in that area were at hand to help them. The army of the English was then small, owing to the absence of the king, who at the time was attending to the obsequies of his brother. Although the ranks were not at full strength, high courage was in their breasts, and rejoicing in battle they repel the enemy some distance. However, overcome with weariness, they desist from fighting, and the barbarians won a degree of victory which one might call fruitless.

871 Ashdown and the Year of the Great Battles

Supposing the descendant of Æthelred *was* right, this latest battle might represent the first flexing of the muscle of the newly arrived fleet. If Alfred had not already gazed into the faces of the leaders of the new Danish reinforcements, then by now he will have been only too aware of their presence in Wessex. Among them was the man who would haunt the young king of Wessex for many years. His name was Guthrum.

Tradition dictated that the period of mourning for a king should last a whole month. There was a set sequence to this sombre ritual of *month's mind*, and it will have been strictly observed by Alfred. So much so, that it is not surprising, perhaps, that Asser says it was a full month after Alfred's accession that the war resumed. 'Almost unwillingly', he says, Alfred went into battle. Alfred later claimed that he had not unduly sought out his role as earthly ruler, perhaps to placate those who thought he had intrigued and pushed for what was clearly a lofty position of temporal power. But at this stage in his career, there is something of the reluctant hero about Asser's favourite Englishman.

A hero at Ashdown, perhaps, but now the responsibilities of kingship were deeper than those of an heir to the throne. And the news that reached him way down south in Wimborne was awful. The Danes were in full array yet again. Reading had moved en masse with a fresh heart and new limbs. Its target, perhaps predictably, was another royal manor – another attempted knock-out blow to remove the last of the line of Æthelwulf and thus pave the way for a Danish kingdom. A force no smaller than the original Great Heathen Army of 865 had struck out with full confidence for Wilton, deep in the heart of Alfred's kingdom.

On the hill at Wilton, along the southern side of the banks of the River Wylye, another curious battle was fought. Alfred met the full force of the Great Heathen Army with just a handful of desperate, courageous men. The scene is quite imaginable. A desperate scramble for their horses at Wimborne, under king's orders, the leading thegns and ealdormen of Wessex sent mounted messengers ahead to their shires for urgent reinforcements. To Wilton they rode with haste.

The Viking Wars of Alfred the Great

We do not know how Alfred managed it with such a small force, but his men smashed into the entire Danish army with such ferocity that they were unable to withstand the onslaught. Slowly they gave way to the attacking English until, what seemed like a recoil, became a retreat. Alfred's heart must have leapt. His first battle as king and he had sent the enemy reeling, just like at Ashdown. And here there was fresh blood on the enemy side, yet still it would be spilled. The battle raged around the small troop of Englishmen. The king's elation soon turned to anguish. Asser claims that, due to their small number (which was attributable to the ravages of the previous battles), the West Saxons were unable to prosecute the rout fully. They may have proved they could win the battlefield argument by tenacity alone, but by attempting to follow up the victory with such a small force they were to be effectively outwitted. Those who chased were swamped by a Danish army that seems to have had the tactical capability to turn on its heels and envelope its pursuers with superior numbers. It was a false dawn for the king. As he observed the ghastly sight of the cream of his own nobility being hacked down in a swarm of heathen men, he knew the Danes would occupy the field of battle and that it would be Alfred himself who would have to retreat and surrender Wilton. Running out of human resources, he would have to think of alternative ways, of desperate ways, to stop the enemy from striking the killer blow against his capital. It was an inauspicious start to a reign. Worse still, the new leaders Guthrum, Anwend and Oscetyl had seen at close quarters the nature of their enemy and they had prevailed against him.

Alfred, often sickly, often quiet, until he was finally stirred into action, had taken the leading men of Wessex to Wilton and for some of them the journey had meant death. An exhausted West Saxon aristocracy could be forgiven for harbouring dark thoughts about their new lord, especially those who felt their allegiance to lie naturally with the heirs of Æthelred. But whatever the noblemen were thinking, and whatever the views of a new player on the stage – the questioning archbishop of Canterbury – things would quickly get a good deal worse for the troubled monarch.

871 Ashdown and the Year of the Great Battles

London, Winter 871–872

It was time for reflection. The year was only halfway through and already Alfred had ridden to countless battles, in which he had either harassed his enemy when it was out foraging or had met the whole Danish army in the field. He had lost valuable men and had seen great leaders fall on either side, and yet his problem was no smaller now than it had been on the morning of the battle of Ashdown. Perhaps both sides realised they could no longer continue to fight each other to a standstill, but it seems to have been Alfred who made the first move, and in the long run, it nearly did for him.

Charles the Bald had done it in Francia, almost as a matter of regular policy. Whenever the Frankish king had paid the Vikings their tribute money, Charles's enemies seemed temporarily to disappear – at least until such time as they thought it beneficial to break their agreement with him. But by that time Charles will have gambled on having bought enough weeks or months to build new fortifications and attend to other military needs. For Alfred, although this was clearly going to be expensive, it was necessary for him now to buy time. The *Anglo-Saxon Chronicle* says that, at this time, the West Saxons 'made peace' with the Danes, implying there was a cash settlement. But it was not the money itself that was Alfred's problem, it was how he raised it. There is evidence to suggest that the king coerced his nobles and bishops to find the money, and for those who could not do so, their land would be forfeited to the king, who paid their share. Alfred's estates would grow as a result of what, to the aristocracy and the Church, must have seemed like an unduly punitive policy. It all left a good deal of resentment among the men who had fought long and hard earlier in the year to rid Wessex of the pagan menace. For the churchmen it seemed doubly cruel. They were now being stripped of their wealth by both pagan and Christian alike. The community at Abingdon, which suffered great depredations at the hands of the heathens, still found enough resentment in their hearts to implicate the 'Judas' Alfred when they put quill to paper. But if Abingdon was smouldering in discontent rather than Danish fires, there was someone else in the Church that had great misgivings about the king's new approach. Alfred would come to realise the extent of Canterbury's discomfort.

Amid a mountain of silver, Halfdan and Guthrum sat at Reading and pondered their next move. They had promised to leave Wessex, but where should they go? Certainly, their attack on Wessex brought them great riches, but had not dislodged its monarch, despite numerous battles. Guthrum, in particular, paid great attention to this one important fact. The strength of Alfred's grip on his kingdom fascinated him. The Dane looked for signs of weakness and saw it not on the battlefield, but in the halls and homesteads of the countryside. For now, Guthrum would go with Halfdan, and together they would honour their promise. After all, there was one kingdom left to try: a kingdom to whose historical power the Great Heathen Army had perhaps given too much deference. Burgred's kingdom, once the flower of Christian Europe under King Offa, was a pale shadow of its former self. Because of a long history of dynastic struggles in this vast kingdom, Burgred was nothing like as firmly fixed on his throne as Alfred, nor was he as rich. The opportunity for long-term gains in Mercia was just too tempting for the Danes. And so they sailed down the Thames to the burgeoning Mercian port of Lundenwic. Here, over the winter, they divided their spoils and bagged their share of trading income coming through the port.

From London, the Danish leadership could keep its finger on the political pulse of both Wessex and Mercia. If Alfred had fought when he could and paid well when he could not, the same could not be said of Burgred. The Mercian king seemed only too willing to treat with the enemy at the earliest opportunity. His paucity in finances could not offset his unwillingness to meet the enemy in the field. At London, the Danes began calling in their Mercian tribute money, and it was the devil's job for Burgred to raise it. Alfred and Wessex had survived – just.

The withering intimidation of Mercia left a memory deep in the hearts of the men associated with the port of London and with their Mercian sponsors. A surviving document tells how Wærferth, the bishop of Worcester, was forced to sell some of his estates to one of Burgred's thegns for a colossal amount of silver. The money raised went straight to London and to the Heathen Army. This is just one recorded incident in what must have been a forlorn procession of cartloads of tribute heading for London in 872. But then, in the autumn of that year, a messenger came to the settlement with bad news: not so bad for the long-suffering Londoners, but rather for Halfdan. The arrangements that he had made for the government of Northumbria in his absence were in tatters. The story told to him was one of a great disturbance in the city of York. Ecgberht and his archbishop, Wulfhere, the pliant clients of the new Scandinavian north, had been overthrown. Someone had at last taken a dislike to Viking rule.

872 Rebellion at York

A Danish Base at Torksey

A brand-new set of objectives now presented themselves to the Danes. They knew they had to deal swiftly with the Northumbrian uprising and re-establish stability in the land where they might eventually come to settle. Wessex would not feature in their designs for the rest of this year or even the next. Alfred, for his part, kept himself informed. His scouts and informants told him of how the Danes had set themselves a camp at Torksey, in Lincolnshire, just to the north-east of Lincoln. Torksey was an important strategic settlement in the ancient kingdom of Lindsey, whose ruling elite had only melted through intermarriage into Mercia within the last few generations. It was positioned at the junction of the Trent and an ancient Roman canal giving access to Lincoln. From here, York, East Anglia and Nottingham were accessible. It was the perfect choice. But Alfred must have feared that Torksey could be Burgred's Reading. What Alfred would not have guessed, perhaps, is how the Mercian king, who was married to his own sister, would react to threat.

It must have satisfied the Danish leadership at Torksey to have learned that Burgred had given shelter to the now-exiled Ecgberht and Wulfhere. Perhaps he thought this single act was appeasement enough for the Danes and that he might be spared their close attention. But the Danes had a plan for Burgred and it was designed to break him.

Firmly established at Torksey, the Danes dealt with the Northumbrian uprising swiftly, presumably by sending a detachment of an appropriate size to the city. We know little about the campaign and less still why it was an Englishman called Ricsige whom the Scandinavians elevated to the throne and not Ecgberht, who may have recently died. The little we know is enough: Danish rule through a puppet king had been quickly re-established at York. Wulfhere, the archbishop whose correspondence with the pope reveals Rome's curious acceptance that there were pagans ruling this great northern Christian city was returned, once again, to work alongside the heathens.

With stability restored in York, the kingdom would be managed again in the way the leadership wished: Halfdan wanted it kept open for him and his followers to settle the land when he was ready. But he was not ready. Torksey had been chosen as a base for a good reason and that reason would become apparent to Burgred. Why had they not all gone to York? That city, given its recent truculence, would have been the ideal place for the Danes to spend the winter of 872–873. Why were they hovering over him?

The Danes called in their tribute payments from an increasingly depleted Mercia while they were at Torksey. Throughout the year of 873 Burgred realised they would not stop bleeding him dry. But the Danes did indeed leave Torksey. If, through his painful payments, Burgred thought that he had managed to secure their departure from his kingdom, as he had done at Nottingham years ago, then his heart must have broken when he found out where they had gone.

873 Repton: The End of Independent Mercia

The Death of Ivarr

By sailing down the Trent to Repton and infesting the sacred Mercian royal mausoleum there, the Danish leadership was delivering a message they might have thought about doing at Wimborne. All of Burgred's enemies lay at Repton. The latest additions to the enemies of Burgred were the living and breathing Danes, but the dead Englishmen buried there haunted the Mercian ruler too. Both the living and the dead of Repton represented an unpleasant apparition to a man who, now thoroughly depressed, had to suffer the ignominy of psychological defeat. It was Viking warfare at its most devastating. Not a single spear would be thrown in anger while Burgred lost a war.

The church of St Wystan in Repton – around which the Danes

Repton

When the Great Heathen Army took over the Mercian royal centre at Repton in 873 it is possible that they brought to this place the body of Ivarr 'beinlauss' – 'the boneless'. Ivarr, after a successful initial campaign with his brothers in England had gone to Ireland and had died there. Excavations at Repton have revealed that in a cut down mortuary chapel beneath a pagan burial mound lay the body of a tall man surrounded by the bones of about 200 men of military age. The sagas tell us that Ivarr was not known for his compassion and that throughout his life he remained childless:

'he was formed in such a way that neither lust nor love was part of his nature, but he was not lacking in wisdom or ferocity. He died of old age in England [sic] and was buried there in a howe.'

Confusion over the ailment which troubled Ivarr has remained for centuries. Some say he may have suffered from a brittle-bone disease which supports some sagas' insistence that he had to be carried around everywhere on his shield, whilst others take a more pragmatic view. There is a chance that the tall and important Dane interred beneath the mound at Repton is indeed Ivarr, son of Ragnar and tormentor of the Christian kingdoms of England.

erected a remarkable D-shaped ditch and bank, using the church itself as a sort of gatehouse – held Mercian memories in its crypt. That crypt, which still survives to this day, attracted pilgrims from all over Anglo-Saxon England, who came to file past the relics of St Wigstan and to honour the remains of other Mercian kings. But the cult of St Wigstan was an uncomfortable one for Burgred. His own dynastic line (often referred to as the Mercian 'B' dynasty) was not affiliated with those who lay at Repton. In fact, it was quite the opposite. Halfdan knew that if he claimed this place as his own, a message of overwhelming potency would be delivered across the land. Halfdan was here to remind Burgred that, despite his long reign, he had no real right to the throne. The Danes were trying to make their own claim look legitimate. In this special place they began to bury their own dead in their own fashion. It was a psychological masterstroke.

Of all the hundreds of Danish dead at Repton, one large man in a central grave has attracted the attention of archaeologists and historians alike. Æthelweard's assertion that Ivarr had died in the same year as St Edmund is at variance with other evidence. The Irish annals for the year 872/3 state that Ivarr 'the king of the northmen of all Ireland and Britain' was dead. Scandinavian legend has it that Ivarr was buried somewhere in England 'under a howe' or burial mound. If the large body found recently at Repton by archaeologists in the paganised chapel (which was covered with earth in 873) is Ivarr, it would make a lot of sense. Vikings are known to have gone to extraordinary lengths to retrieve their dead leaders for interment. To have placed the dead Ivarr here at Repton, amid the remains of the Old Mercian Royal order, is to suggest that political continuity in Mercia would pass from Wigstan's dynasty to the Danes, thus bypassing Burgred's line.

For the Mercian king – Alfred's brother-in-law – it had all been too much. He took his wife Æthelswith and fled his kingdom, forever leaving the island of Britain. He had reigned for over two decades. He had fought battles against the Welsh and for the most part protected his kingdom well. But he was soon to end his life cold and broken after a long journey, which took him through Pavia, where Alfred and Æthelred had stayed as young pilgrims on a very different journey so many years before. Burgred's body was laid to rest not in any Mercian royal mausoleum, but in St Mary's Church in the English Quarter in Rome, his tomb a permanent reminder of the effectiveness of the Viking art of war.

In place of Burgred, the Danes chose to promote a man to the throne whose dynastic affiliations had been firmly bound up with the enemies of the former king. The *Anglo-Saxon Chronicle* records the ascent to power in Mercia of Ceolwulf II 'a foolish king's thegn'. He was a half-brother of St Wigstan, and with such royal blood pumping through his veins, he would have been deemed acceptable to Mercians. But the terms of his tenure are likely to have been equally as onerous as those suffered by the puppet rulers of the north. Ceolwulf had to swear oaths and promise to keep his kingdom open for the Danes whenever they wished to have it. He would also bring to bear his own military following when his political masters called for it. For Asser, the agreement was a 'wretched' one. As the news of Ceolwulf's accession and the abdication of his brother-in-law reached Alfred, he will have had to make a choice. Should he work with the new king or reject him as a usurper? It seems he chose the former option, despite the fact that his own sister had paid such a price for Ceolwulf's rise to power. Ceolwulf and Alfred are known to have shared coin strikers (men who were sanctioned to produce silver coinage on behalf of their king) and perhaps they also shared other forms of governmental administration during Ceolwulf's reign.

874 The Danes Split Forces

Throughout 874 the Danes sat in triumph. Should they now settle in Mercia and call in the favours owed by Ceolwulf? Had they finished their war of conquest now that Northumbria, East Anglia and Mercia had fallen to them? There was much to discuss around the burning fires of Repton that year. Halfdan will have argued to Guthrum that Ivarr's death had left a political vacuum in the north and that it was necessary for Halfdan to fill it on behalf of his late brother. He was right.

The Viking Wars of Alfred the Great

Ivarr had been active in the north during 871 but when he died, Eysteinn, the son of Olaf the White had taken control of Viking Ireland and this, more than anything else, would have irked his brother. Guthrum, no son of Ragnar, who had arrived on the scene in England as late as 871, had brought with him a set of people whose expectations seem to have been slightly different from those of the original campaigners, the veterans of the first Great Heathen Army of the autumn of 865. Guthrum, Anwend and Oscetyl had thrown themselves into the fray against the one kingdom that had fought them all to a standstill, and for a man like Guthrum, this must have left an uncomfortable feeling. His followers would need him to settle his own political scores and not simply aid the sons of Ragnar in their own campaigns. It was obvious to Guthrum that, for his own survival, he must defeat the tenacious king south of the River Thames. For this however, he needed a plan.

Ingelby – The Parting of the Ways

On rising ground to the south side of the Trent Valley about 3 miles south-east of the Danish camp at Repton lies a pagan Viking cemetery in Heath Wood, Ingelby. It differs in nature from the Scandinavian burials at Repton in that the majority of the 59 barrows seem to have been cremation burials with one or two possible cenotaphs marking the exception. Two damaged swords and the cremated remains of humans, ox, horse, sheep, pig and dog point to the playing out of an elaborate pagan sacrifice near to the spiritual heart of a Christian kingdom.

It may be the case that when the Great Heathen Army chose to split its forces and operate in different parts of Britain, that part of it which was perhaps led by Guthrum decided to bury its recent dead not at Repton where the sons of Ragnar had already staked their psychological claim over the Mercians, but at Ingelby. Here, they could indulge in their pagan rites before moving south to Cambridge and thence to conquer Wessex.

875 Wareham

By the autumn of 874 the combined forces of Danish Repton agreed to split. Halfdan, who had already indicated his fears for the Scandinavian north, took his veterans to Northumbria, along with the forces of his brother Ubba, where, between them, they began a war of subjugation and conquest from a new base on the River Tyne, picking up where Ivarr had left off, battling against the Strathclyders and Picts. Halfdan was concerned that the Clyde corridor, which linked Northumbria to Scandinavian-controlled Ireland, had been closed in the recent upheavals. His campaigns were to be centred on reopening this route and his obsession with Dublin would one day cost him his life, when he was ambushed on Strangford Lough by his Norwegian political enemies. But our attention must now turn to the man who took his army from Repton to seek quite a different fortune. Guthrum marched his army south, not to Wessex as one might expect, but to settle for a while in East Anglia. Guthrum and his army had come to Cambridge.

875 Wareham

The Plan of Guthrum

With the summer of 875 came dreaded news of sails on the horizon, somewhere off the coast of Wessex. Nobody knows who commanded these vessels or who sent them to the waters of Alfred's kingdom. All we know is the chronicler's account that 'King Alfred went out to sea with a ship force and fought against seven shiploads, and captured one of them and put the others to flight.' The capture of that one vessel may be of significance. The Danes had been masters of the sea for a long time. The reasons for their supremacy lay largely in the skill of their sailors and in the design of their vessels. Long, shallow-draft, keel-built ships, capable of both traversing the high seas and of infiltrating river systems deep in land. Alfred will have taken a keen interest in his prize. Already successful in this recent naval encounter, he must have now begun formulating ideas as to how to improve his naval capability based on the design of enemy ships. But the Alfred of 875 was not yet the man history would remember. Forward planning, as yet, does not seem to have been a conspicuous aspect of West Saxon government. Alfred, despite having had four years of relative peace in which to bolster the defences of his kingdom, seems to have done very little in this respect. Soon, a vengeful and lustful enemy would once again fall on Wessex with an armoury of tricks at its disposal, and all the English king would have to withstand it would be the same resources he used to avoid defeat the last time it had happened. But Alfred's problem was that those resources were his own people, and people, as he would soon discover, have memories.

The winter of 875 saw Guthrum launch the first phase of his plan. The surviving accounts of it are interesting. The Danes, according to Asser, left Cambridge 'by night'. It is almost as if they were being watched. But if they were indeed being observed by West Saxon scouts in the vicinity of Cambridge, the *Anglo-Saxon Chronicle*'s statement that the Danes 'stole away from the West Saxon army into Wareham' will have come as a humiliation to everyone on the English side, not least to the leaders of the hastily gathered fyrd and to Alfred himself. Wareham is around 130 miles from Cambridge and it would have taken Guthrum's land army a full four days at least to get there. His guile was matched by his stealth in the landscape.

Guthrum already had experience of battling against the West Saxon fyrdsmen. He could not have struck out across country from Cambridge with the express intent of bringing a giant army to battle, especially as he had experienced the cost of such warfare at close quarters. His plan was to slip past the Anglo-Saxons while pursuing a different goal, and this he was successful in doing. The goal was Wareham. Wareham was a vital cross-Channel port on the Dorset coast. Guthrum had cut a swathe through the heart of Wessex to get there and he had done so with a land army. Alfred's confused fyrdsmen had to play catch-up with Guthrum, but it was too late. The enemy had ensconced itself behind the defences of the town.

But why had Guthrum chosen Wareham in the first place? Not only was it a settlement with a nunnery, farm and portable wealth in the form of trading goods, it also had a geography

875 Wareham

suitable for natural defence, whereby the Rivers Frome and Tarrant swirled their way around the town, enclosing an area large enough to graze animals. But hidden beneath the words of the ancient texts, there may be another reason for Guthrum's choice. We do not know exactly what was discussed between the Ragnarsons and Guthrum before the parting of the ways at Repton, but we do know that in the far west of Britain – the part which is closest to the most important parts of central Wessex – the Cornish had bided their time in anticipation of revenge against the line of Ecgberht. If Guthrum could take Wareham at the eastern end of the Wessex heartland and the Cornish invade (with Danish help) from the west, then the final knockout blow might be delivered from the north by an invasion somewhere along the coast of Somerset or Devon. The problem, as we shall see, with all such plans was in the timing: if any one part of it failed, it might all fail. And one small part had already faltered: Halfdan was dead. It would fall to Ubba, his brother to fulfil the role on the northern front, but he was busy away in the northern lands.

So, as the Anglo-Saxons began laying siege to their own settlement, they might have thought that they had their prey after all. Guthrum had surely come too far into Wessex to get away with anything. Here he was holed-up in the deep south with an English army preparing to starve him out. But this notion will have been shattered by the news that 120 enemy sail were even now sailing around the coast of Kent and heading up the English Channel.

The identity of the occupants of these vessels is not certain, nor is the identity of those who led them. They are likely to have been Guthrum's own force of shipmen, the Danish leader having chosen to launch a combined operation by land and by sea to reach his target at Wareham. What is certain, however, is that these people would have numbered in their thousands, and would have brought with them supplies, transport and manpower. With these additional troops, Guthrum would have been able to prosecute his plan. He would survive the winter and push out into Wessex at a time of his choosing to finally crush the West Saxon king. Wessex would be under Danish control.

The Viking Wars of Alfred the Great

876 The Oath Breaker

Divine Intervention

With 120 ships soon to be anchored in Poole harbour, Alfred had to decide what to do quickly. The strategy he came up with reveals a man keen to try something new, and keen enough to learn something about his enemy. Alfred remembered how, after Wilton, an agreement had been made, backed up by the credible threat of further warfare, and that the Danes had indeed left his kingdom and had stayed away for four years. The king needed to convince Guthrum that his army was big enough, strong enough, and determined enough to thwart the Dane, whatever his next move. He had to convince Guthrum that he was cornered. But extracting a promise to leave from a Viking was no easy task. Burgred had found to his cost that the Danes thought nothing of reneging on an agreement when it suited them, so Alfred had to be careful that what happened next did not turn into a costly charade.

Alfred needed a binding agreement. This would not be a 'Nottingham'. Nor would Wareham become the West Saxon king's Torksey. Previous agreement had, of course, been bound by hostage exchanges, where each side chose important members from its number and swapped them into their enemy's hands for assurance that the agreement would stick. Wareham would be no different in this respect. However, Alfred had spotted that the oaths the heathens had previously sworn upon Christian relics had meant next to nothing to them. He had learned this not only from events in England, but from countless tales of treachery and double-dealing from the Vikings' travels in Francia. The Danes must swear to leave Wessex, not by taking an oath on Christian relics, but by taking an oath on their own sacred holy ring, probably an arm ring, a phenomenon which the *Anglo-Saxon Chronicle* tells us 'earlier they would not do to any nation'. Thus the agreement was made, presumably with Alfred himself swearing oaths on the Christian relics and Guthrum making his promise on his holy ring in front of an assembled mass. It cannot have lacked gravitas and significance. Alfred, as he withdrew from the meeting,

---

Hostages

Hostages were used as a way of securing a peaceful agreement between antagonists. In the era of Alfred, it was often the case that his enemies cared less about what happened to the people they had placed into the care of the English than the English did about the Danes they had in their own care. The Danes' callous disregard for their own hostages annoyed Alfred and the Anglo-Saxons to the extent that when he was in the high ascendancy during the wars, the English king demanded that he should choose hostages from the Danes himself and that there should be no exchange the other way. Such was the case after the battle of Edington in 878. When truces or peace agreements were broken by one side or another, the fate of the hostages was often grim. Sometimes, just as a signal of defiance as was shown by Guthrum to Alfred in 876 at Wareham hostages would be murdered in cold blood before the Danes moved out to another area.

---

might reasonably have thought he had triumphed through diplomacy, a kingdom once again saved by the cleverness of its monarch. But there is one troubling reference in one important source. Æthelweard says that payment was made to the Danes. Perhaps this was the sweetener that clinched the Danes' departure from Wareham. If it is true, it would have come at a heavy price. But regardless of how much silver had been raised to pay off the Danes, resentment in the countryside would be profound. This had not, after all, been the first time. Could not the king think of anything else other than bleeding his compatriots and churchmen of money and other riches just to rid himself of a menace he should be standing up to?

The year rolled on and it became clear that Guthrum had no intention of keeping his side of the agreement. As Halfdan's men began settling in Northumbria, metaphorically turning their swords into ploughshares and forever changing the ethnic and political make-up of that northern kingdom, Guthrum, still quite determined to win a kingdom of his own, ordered his men to mount their horses and steal out of Wareham under cover of darkness. The English army might have been awakened by the screams of their countrymen, as the Danes callously murdered their hostages that night before leaving Wareham. One must assume that a similar fate befell those important Danes given to Alfred in the Wareham agreement. But leaving the kingdom was far from their minds, as they rode out to the west and came to Exeter, an old Roman city known once as Isca, which still had stout defences around it. A Danish alliance with the disaffected Britons of the west did now seem a likely outcome. Once again, Alfred could not catch them before they had reached their destination. Something was seriously wrong with the way the English army was being deployed. Its enemy was running rings around it. From Exeter, Guthrum could do it all again. He might even be able to solicit the aid of those Cornishmen who remembered with bitterness the conquest their fathers had suffered under Alfred's own grandfather.

And so Guthrum sat in Exeter laughing to himself. But what of the fleet of ships in Poole harbour? As Alfred began his chase to Exeter, that fleet was weighing anchor and setting sail to join Guthrum in the west. And then something remarkable happened. No more than 5 or 6 miles into their voyage, off the headland near Swanage, amid what appears to have been a great storm combined with a mist, the entire fleet was lost with all hands. Once the fleet had sailed past the protection of the headland, it must have met the full force of the often dangerous south-westerlies so common in the English Channel. A scene of horror of near biblical proportions unfolded before the eyes of the shore bound locals, a scene which is still commemorated to this day. Somewhere at the bottom of the English Channel, off the coast at Swanage, lie some 3,500 Danish bodies.

Exeter

Guthrum was dismayed to hear about the fate of the ships. There he was in Exeter, having broken his promise, and as of yet he had paid no price for it. But now he had to continue without thousands of well armed men. Even worse, now an angry Alfred, fully believing in the oaths he had sworn over Christian relics and fully accepting Swanage as a judgement from on High, was now encamped outside the gates of Exeter. The bargaining would have to start all over again, this time with the king of Wessex in a position of strength. Hostages were again given. This time, Alfred made certain that the people given to him were of great enough eminence in the dark heart of the Danish leader to deter him from breaking his promise to leave the kingdom. The *Anglo-Saxon Chronicle* records that the Dane gave him 'as many hostages as he wished to receive', indicating that Alfred was indeed in the ascendancy and that the horrors of Wareham were less likely to repeat themselves.

877 Sedition and Intrigue

Gloucester and the Settling of Mercia

With a new set of promises extracted, backed with a more deeply binding hostage agreement, Alfred expected Guthrum to vacate Exeter soon. The exact sequence of events for the year 877 is difficult to piece together, since Asser leaves out the entire year's entry in his biography. Other sources inform us that by harvest time 877 Guthrum had indeed left Exeter and gone into Mercia, where, in the style of Halfdan, he began sharing out the lands of the ancient English kingdom, granting some of it to its erstwhile caretaker, Ceolwulf II. But what are we missing in the accounts of the crucial year of 877? What clandestine visits to the Danes at Exeter were made by the seditious thegns of Wessex? Therein lay the heart of Alfred's problem. Come Christmas, he would know only too well.

History only obliquely records the conspirators, as we shall shortly discover. Even Æthelweard, himself descended from the line of Alfred's brother and who was thus related to the child about whom so much treacherous attention was focused, could not directly implicate the guilty West Saxons. By the time Æthelweard was writing, in the later tenth century, the right of the line of Alfred to rule over lowland Britain had been spectacularly established. Through the efforts of Alfred's children and grandchildren the Danish Midlands had slowly been militarily clawed back into southern English hands. Æthelweard wrote after Alfred's son, Edward the Elder, received the submission of the rulers of the north in 921, after Alfred's daughter Æthelflæd, 'the Lady of the Mercians', had taken the Danish midland settlements of Derby and Leicester, after Alfred's magnificent grandson, Athelstan, had crushed Scandinavian and Scottish opposition at the lost field of Brunanburh in 937. He wrote, too, after the golden Anglo-Saxon Age, when King Edgar (959–975) presided over a Britain cowed to the rule of Alfred the Great's issue. So, perhaps, it is no surprise that those who conspired to destroy the greatest Englishman in all of the country's history, were very quickly spirited out of the record.

But first to the arrangement with Ceolwulf. The negotiations for the division of Mercia were carried out at Gloucester, where Æthelweard says the Danes had 'pitched their tents'. Guthrum had chosen Gloucester to give him options. It was situated in a place where his allies could reach him, and it was placed neatly above the gap between the Rivers Thames and Avon, into which a southern thrust might prove telling. The west of Mercia, with the exception of Gloucester, was to be given to Ceolwulf, while the whole of the east would be divided among Guthrum's men. Ceolwulf probably also relinquished the traditional Mercian control over London, thus providing the Danes with an important source of income. It was a division that would culturally and legally split central England in two for centuries to come, giving rise, ultimately, to the notion that beyond Watling Street to the north lay a land known as the Danelaw, where judicial practices were different from those in the south. Even after the English conquests of the tenth century these areas retained this curious Anglo-Danish flavour.

It may have comforted Alfred to have learned that Guthrum's choice to settle had at last been made outside his kingdom, and that, perhaps, he could enjoy a period of peace. News of Halfdan's fate will have heartened him also. But the thought of Guthrum hovering above Wessex at Gloucester ought to have troubled Alfred. Instead, the king of Wessex, who was showing to the world that he had an uncanny knack for survival, rested on his laurels. As he made his way to the royal vill at Chippenham that Christmas, Alfred looked forward to the festivities that so entranced the Anglo-Saxons at midwinter. His mind turned to the business of the state, to the giving of gifts, and the needs of a kingdom. But if he felt any comfort at all that winter, then it was sorely misplaced.

878 Edington

Here the raiding-army stole away in midwinter after Twelfth Night to Chippenham, and overrode and occupied the land of Wessex, and drove many of the people across the sea, and the greatest part of the others they over-rode – and the people submitted to them – except for Alfred the king, and he with a small troop went with difficulty through the woods and into swamp fastnesses.

Anglo-Saxon Chronicle (B), 878

Twelfth Night, Monday, 6 January 878

In the ninth century Christmas was a quite different affair. The Anglo-Saxon kingdoms of England had been Christian for many centuries and there is no doubting the passion of the devotees in their worship of the Christmas miracle. But this was Yuletide as well. In fact, the celebration on the night of 25 December of the birth of Jesus Christ had only been fully ratified at the Synod of Chelsea in 816. Behind all this lay a tradition steeped in the pagan mists, wrapped within the notion of the desolation of midwinter and the solemn longing for the return of the sun. It was not so long ago that men and women chased down the midwinter sun over the horizon, running along the great prehistoric linear monuments that still litter the English land-scape today; not so long ago when a pagan Saxon goddess, the mother of the sun, was worshipped at this time of year. Upon the ceremonies of feasting, gift-giving, carol-singing, religious processions and firelight displays in the ninth century were comfortably grafted the associated Christian rituals, which brought Jesus Christ into the hearts of the Anglo-Saxon people through the magic of the Mass. Always important, was the observation of the ritual of the twelve nights. In the winter of 877–878, on the last of these nights, a near fatal blow would be delivered to the last free English king of Anglo-Saxon England. It would come in the form of a coup delivered by a pagan enemy on this important holy day.

Every time Guthrum had tried it before, through force of arms, it had led to stalemate. Alfred had just about managed to hold on to his kingdom through a mixture of energy, luck and bribery, thereby denying Guthrum control of the big prize. But this Christmas Guthrum would try a different tack. Aware of the disaffection among the West Saxon witan, and having completed his negotiations with those who would betray their king while sharing his Christmas feast, Guthrum began to pack away those tents in Gloucester and head south.

Moving once again with stealth, Guthrum 'stole away' to Chippenham, to deliver the coup de grâce. There is no recorded battle. If we are brave enough, we might assume that the gates were left ajar. That night the conspirators had no choice but to reveal themselves, as they told Alfred the game was up. As they entered his hall, their words must have broken the king's heart. Anglo-Saxon witans had the power to unelect kings but rarely used it. Here, in the winter of 877–878, they did just that. Guthrum would stand sponsor to an alternative candidate to the West Saxon throne. We cannot be certain exactly what Guthrum wanted once Alfred was out of the way, although we might be forgiven for assuming that he saw himself as a ruler of both Dane and Englishman everywhere south of the Humber. If this was the case, he now looked as if he might achieve it.

Curiously, Alfred did not perish in the coup. Although the Danish march on Chippenham had led to some of the thegns of Wessex fleeing 'across the sea', the *Anglo-Saxon Chronicle* records how many of them submitted to the Danes. Alfred, for his part, seems either to have narrowly escaped at just the right moment, or was somehow allowed to leave Chippenham by agreement. But if Guthrum thought that Alfred's departure would follow the model laid down by the shattered Burgred, then ultimately he would be confounded.

For four years Alfred had enjoyed a peace of sorts, although he knew only too well how fragile his hold on power really was. During this time he had singularly failed to take preventative measures to deal with what might, for some, have seemed inevitable: the return of the Danes. Fragments of evidence survive pointing to the fact that the king was clearly under pressure in these peaceful years. In 876 one of Alfred's charters of Kent contains a huge list of important witnesses, including Æthelred, the archbishop of Canterbury. And it was with the archbishop that Alfred had the biggest problem.

Archbishop Æthelred represented an institution that was not altogether in harmony with Alfred's family. The king's grandfather, Ecgberht, had secured in 838 various concessions from Canterbury at the Council of Kingston. This had come at a time when the West Saxon juggernaut was in the ascendancy and its king was wresting control of the former Anglo-Saxon kingdoms at the eastern end of its jurisdiction. But even this deep-rooted antagonism was not enough for Canterbury to turn against the king. Æthelred was on good terms with his counterpart in York. Both archbishops received correspondence from Rome. The pope was alarmed to hear from the archbishop of Canterbury of Alfred's actions against the Church and was moved to write directly to the king about it. In a letter written to the archbishop by the pope, he goes as far as suggesting that Æthelred steel himself for some difficult times ahead in his struggle with the king, but that he could rest assured that Canterbury would have Rome behind it. As far as the archbishop was concerned, he had looked at the experience of York and had concluded that an archbishop could thrive under Danish rule. All was not lost to the devil, after all.

So, with a small group of friends, a forlorn king was led to the door of his own vill at Chippenham and flung into an unforgiving winter landscape. But who had held that door open? From their complete absence in witness lists of the reign of

The Viking Wars of Alfred the Great

Alfred after 878, it is clear there were a number of potential conspirators. Whether or not they had the full backing of the archbishop of Canterbury is unclear. Cuthred of Hampshire, Ælfstan of Dorset, Mucel, Eadwulf and Milred disappear at this time, as does the bishop of Winchester, who might also be implicated. But there is one whose fate was recalled some twenty-two years later in a charter of Alfred's son, King Edward the Elder (900–924). In 901 Edward gave ten hides of land to one Æthelwulf beside the River Wylye in Wiltshire, formerly owned by one Wulfhere, which, it was said, were forfeited by Wulfhere and his wife on account of treason. Wulfhere is described as having deserted his king and his country. This may indicate that Wulfhere was among the many who fled in the aftermath of Chippenham to Francia, or it may indicate that Wulfhere's treason was in a far more direct form than simple desertion. What is noticeable about these potential conspirators is their affinity with the line of Alfred's brother, the late king Æthelred I, and not with Alfred himself. It could just be the case that they were supporting the claim of the young Æthelwold, King Æthelred's eldest son, under Danish sponsorship. If this was the case, it is all the more remarkable that the chronicler Æthelweard does not mention such a thing, given that he was descended from Æthelred I himself. By the late tenth century the right of the line of Alfred to rule had been so successfully established that it was probably deemed best to forget about the treachery of 878.

Just how small this band of unhappy but loyal followers of the deposed king really was is evidenced by the pen of Æthelweard. Alfred took with him 'no other reinforcements except servants who had royal maintenance'. It was a truly desperate time. The king slipped away to the west with nowhere to go. Eventually, he would come to Athelney. These months in the wilderness would see Alfred become the raider, attacking patrolling Danes with his small band to seize enough to live on. Once a king, now a refugee, Alfred was a virtual outlaw in his own kingdom, sometimes even robbing his own people to survive. But as the king wearily trod his way through the icy mud in the unforgiving winter forests of Somerset, he

878 Edington

was unaware of a force sailing from South Wales, whose sole intention it seemed was to work with Guthrum in finally delivering the killer blow to Anglo-Saxon Wessex and thereby bringing to an abrupt end a whole period of English history.

Cynuit: *The Raven is Taken*

The South Welsh kingdom of Dyfed had been feeling the force of the ravages of the man who had slain King Edmund in 869. Ubba had probably seen his brother fall in Ireland, but had reunited with Guthrum to discuss plans for the conquest of Alfred's Wessex. His instruction from Guthrum would have been to position himself so he could strike at Athelney from the Bristol Channel. Some say he came from Wales to the North Devon coast with thirty ships, others say twenty-three. As Guthrum moved south to decapitate the Anglo-Saxon state, Ubba had set sail for the West Country to trap what was left of Alfred's puny force in a hammer-and-anvil move that would see England fall truly into the Scandinavian lap. But it must have been recognised by both Guthrum and Ubba that the wilderness into which Alfred had vanished was, in fact, an area of traditional strength for him. There were still some loyal subjects from these parts, and soon Alfred would team up with one in particular. Æthelnoth, the ealdorman of Somerset had himself been 'lurking in a certain wood with a small force'. The wood is thought to have been at Somerton, just a mile or so east of Athelney. This man's contribution to his king's survival – and therefore to the survival of England as a nation – is difficult to underestimate. It was Eanwulf, ealdorman of Somerset (almost certainly Æthelnoth's father and predecessor) who had shown a young Alfred around the marshlands of Somerset. He had probably led him to the site of his own victory over the Vikings in 845 at the mouth of the Parret, possibly even discussing tactics with him. And here, now, was Æthelnoth, equally converse with the countryside of the west and equally ready to defeat the enemies of Alfred. He would be at the king's side through these cold months; he would share in the semi-legends that grew around the fortification they would together build at Athelney. But as Ubba's ships set their sails for the River Parret

73

and thence to Athelney, there was someone else whom Alfred had a good cause to thank.

The sight that met Ealdorman Odda's eyes when he looked across the Bristol Channel to the north must have filled him with dismay. But he was not a man to give up on his lord. Ubba's ships sailed straight for the Parret estuary. But Ealdorman Odda was sitting in an ancient hillfort overlooking this river, which Asser calls *Cynuit*, and which is most likely to have been the hillfort at Cannington. Asser knew it well, or at least claims to have known it. It was an Iron Age hillfort with ramparts 'thrown up in our style', says the Welshman, in a reference to the ancient British way of doing things. Sometimes *Cynuit* is identified with Countisbury Hill, further west along

Athelney

In Alfred's time Athelney was like an island in the marshes of Somerset linked by a causeway to East Lyng. It was situated on the Tone, a tributary of the River Parret. In early 878 Alfred retreated to Athelney Island virtually as an exile in his own kingdom. From here tales spread about the king and his visions of saints and other miraculous happenings. In reality, Alfred was able to build dwellings and a forge from which he and his remaining followers equipped themselves for the forthcoming assault of the Dane Guthrum's position to the north at Chippenham.

The Somerset levels were ideal territory for guerrilla warfare. Before he was ready to go into battle against the Danes, Alfred with his small band used the trackways of the marshes and forests of Somerset to ambush and harass the patrolling Danes. But sooner or later he would need to move against his enemy with force. This he would be able to do if his loyal forces to the west continued to protect him on that western flank and at the mouth of the Parret and also if he could summon enough of the remaining shires who were not under Danish submission.

the Devonshire coast. This is largely due to Asser's description, and his assertion that he had been to *Cynuit* himself and seen the difficulty of the place. Countisbury Hill may well have been used during this period by the Devonshire fyrdsmen, but Cannington, overlooking the river approaches to the king's wintry hideout, would be an eminently more sensible place to position an army. Whichever of the two candidates was the real *Cynuit*, Odda waited in his defensive position. Ubba's men beached their ships on the shore and undertook a siege. Before them their standard-bearer carried something special, something terrifying to many who were unlucky enough to see it or to feel its anger. The raven was a symbol inextricably linked to pagan Scandinavian mythology. The sons of Ragnar had many sisters, and the *Annals of St Neots* tell us that it was these women who had woven this most famous of Raven banners for their brothers. Picking up on this tale, which was known to him, Sir John Spelman says that the banner was specifically woven for the adventure of avenging the death of Ragnar Lothbrok and had been made almost in an instant by the women. Moreover, it had magical properties:

> [It would] always seem to clap the wings and do as if it would fly but toward the Approach of mishap it would hang right down and not move.

If it is true to say that, generally, the Vikings had no stomach for protracted sieges, then it is equally true to say that Ealdorman Odda of Devon liked them even less. When he landed, Ubba seemed convinced that Odda would eventually run out of water in his lofty retreat, where there were no springs. After starving him out, Ubba would be free to continue down the Parret towards his ultimate goal. But Odda could not stand to be holed-up for too long. So he adopted a tactic once employed by those Danes who were trapped at Reading, and decided to launch a surprise attack on his besiegers. It was a high-risk strategy, and indicates that Odda knew only too well what was at stake, but it seems to have worked. The plan was to head straight for the banner and the Danish leader. The sources record the loss of 800 Danes and, more importantly, the death of Ubba, one of the sons of Ragnar, a man who had brought misery to the English kingdoms. Finally, one of these terrible men had fallen on English soil and just at this moment, in the dark early months of 878, an Englishman stood over the shattered corpses of a formidable Viking warrior and his forty-strong hearth troop, clutching their sacred banner, now hanging lifeless in the breeze. There was hope at last. As for that famous banner, Spelman neatly sums up its fate:

> What so ever it was, the imposture was now betrayed: for being taken by surprise, they had lost their Oracle before they had time to consult with it.

Athelney, Easter 878, Legends and Reality

Æthelnoth knew the landscape of his native Somerset like the back of his hand. This half-starved band of retainers, lowly thegns and servant men and women, seem to have taken heart and soon a plan was hatched, possibly at the behest of the ealdorman, to build up Athelney as a stronghold.

The Somerset Levels were forbidding to anyone. Æthelnoth and his king were situated right in the middle of them. By placing themselves at Athelney, with Odda protecting the northern approaches to the area, the band put itself in a position of defensible strength. At this time, much of the fenland around here was only accessible by boat. Halfway between his old estates of Wedmore and Aller, Alfred began building something approaching a fortress 'of elegant work-manship', reached by a bridge or causeway at both ends. This island in a swamp would be home for a little while longer. Here the band could more readily live off the abundant wildlife and could begin thinking of a plan. By Easter it was finished. Alfred, the exiled king, had one small corner of his kingdom to call his own again. But his time at Athelney was not only full of plan-ning and preparation. It was filled with divine visions of saints, of premonitions, predictions, of anguish and of forgetfulness. Alfred, the last surviving son of Æthelwulf, was staring a

romantic depiction of Dark Age warriors aboard their ships.

Portrait of King Alfred, an engraving of 1661.

A Viking ship at Pegwell Bay, based on a replica of the Gokstad ship.

Ninth-century warrior of Anglo-Saxon England armed with spear and knife. (*Photograph courtesy of John Eagle*)

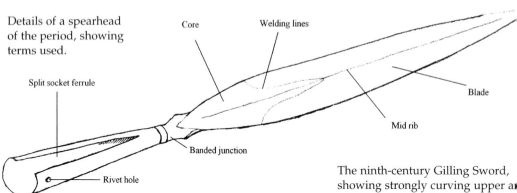

Details of a spearhead of the period, showing terms used.

Core

Welding lines

Split socket ferrule

Blade

Mid rib

Banded junction

Rivet hole

The ninth-century Gilling Sword, showing strongly curving upper an lower pommel guards.

Anglo-Saxon sword pommel from the River Seine in Paris.

nglo-Saxon king and shield-bearer war.

A popular image of Alfred burning the cakes, an allegorical tale from his months in the wilderness.

atue of King Alfred at his birthplace in antage.

York, the centre of the northern world. The Scandinavians sought to link York and Dublin to challenge the power of southern English kings.

The Westbury White Horse supposedly marks the site of the battle of Edington, 878. The Danes were apparently camped here amid the steep ramparts of Bratton Camp.

Built by Henry Hoare between 1762–72 this magnificent tower commemorates the meeting place at Egbert's Stone of the Anglo-Saxon army prior to the battle of Edington, 878.

Alfred the Great as commemorated at the
Temple of British Worthies, Stowe.

KING ALFRED

THE MILDEST JUSTEST, MOST BENEFICENT OF KINGS;

WHO DROVE OUT THE DANES, SECURED THE SEAS, PROTECTED LEARNING

ESTABLISH'D JURIES, CRUSH'D CORRUPTION, GUARDED LIBERTY;

AND, WAS THE FOUNDER OF THE ENGLISH CONSTITUTION.

The Statue of King Alfred stands proud in the ancient West Saxon capital of Winchester.

King Alfred's Castle. Built by Jeremiah Dixon (1726–82) on Tunnel Howe Hill, outside Leeds, as tribute to the king of the Anglo-Saxons. (*Photograp courtesy of Leeds Central Library*)

Statue of Alfred in Trinity Square, Southwark. Reputedly one of the oldest statues in London.

LFRED REX HA
C URBEM FECIT·
NNO   DOMINIC
E INCARNATIO
IS   DCCCLXXX
EGNI   SUI   VIII

ragment of commemorative plaque
rom Shaftesbury.

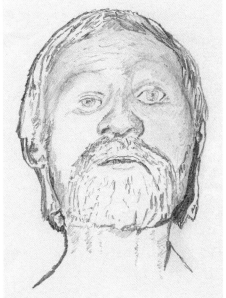

The face of the man from Repton, based on an archaeological reconstruction. This could be Ivarr Ragnarson.

Sculpture of Æthelflæd, Alfred's daughter and the young Athelstan at Tamworth. Between them they would re-conquer the northern world for the Anglo-Saxons. (*Photograph courtesy of Paul Barber*)

Coronation Stone in Kingston, Surrey. The son and grandsons of Alfred were crowned at this famous place in the tenth century.

dream-like obscurity square in the face. It was the stuff of Anglo-Saxon legend and yet it was being played out for real, amid the mists of the Somerset marshes.

A war of sorts was still being fought against the Danes from the Anglo-Saxon base at Athelney. Supported by the people near to Athelney, raids were kept up, but a greater force would be needed if ever Alfred was to dislodge the usurper of Chippenham. He could hardly call on those who had fled overseas, and anyway, how could he be sure they would believe he was still alive? Odda and the men from the west were already engaged in what was proving to be a vital defence of the western and northern flanks. On his sorties from Athelney Alfred pondered the question. One of these outings has remained in the popular imagination for over a thousand years, a remarkable feat for an incident that probably never happened at all. The king who burned the cakes is the abiding epitaph for Alfred, whose real-life achievements deserve so much more than this one curious memory. Historians have worked hard to find the true meaning of the tale, which first appeared in the *Life of St Neot*, written about a hundred years after the exile in Athelney. Their efforts have resulted in a theory that Alfred only metaphorically burned his cakes.

The story goes that Alfred, alone one day in the wilderness, knocked on the door of a lowly local dwelling. Could he seek refuge in this swineherd's house, he asked? The swineherd's wife let her Christian brother into their home and soon the king, who was not recognised by his hosts, had fallen into a dream of intense concentration regarding his predicament. He had not spotted that the bread, or cakes, which his hostess had put in the oven, were burning. The woman ran to the oven and chastised her guest, telling him that he could not be bothered to help her with turning these loaves, but was obviously happy to eat them. Alfred, it is implied, knew she was right. But the whole thing is an allegory. Alfred knew that the concept of failing to attend to business had cost him dear. What had he done to prevent things turning out the way they had? When the Danes had left Wessex after Wilton and gone to dismantle another man's kingdom, the king of Wessex had conspicuously failed to tend to the pressing needs of national defence. Now, at his darkest hour, he was feeling the pain. A successful king should not find himself in the house of his subjects, failing even to attend to the most basic of duties. The author of the *Life of St Neot* knew it, and so did the lonely king of the Somerset swamp. Because it is an allegorical tale, it is perhaps no surprise that at Athelney, St Neot is said to have appeared to Alfred and told him that he would indeed triumph over his enemies. The circle was complete: the admonishment, the guilt, the divine promise of success, all wrapped up in a charming and unforgettable tale.

St Neot was not the only saint who is said to have appeared to the king at Athelney. A mysterious pilgrim somehow entered the fortification while most of its defenders were on a hunting trip and approached the king, begging for alms. Alfred broke into his supplies of wine and bread and shared them with the strange traveller. The symbolism is lost on nobody. The pilgrim took his leave and, strange to say, left behind no hint of a footprint. Alfred returned to his stores, having shared the most precious of supplies in a difficult time, to find the stocks mysteriously replenished. The hunters soon returned with a colossal catch of fish and later that night, as he slept, a vision of a man dressed in bishop's robes appeared before the king and told him that the next day helpers would arrive to aid him in his struggle with his enemies. When questioned by Alfred, the apparition identified himself as none other than St Cuthbert. Simeon of Durham, a later chronicler, has Cuthbert as this saviour, as does the *Winchester Book of Hyde*. In an instant it is possible to see what was happening to the legend of Alfred in the wilderness during the centuries which followed the ninth. The figure ultimately responsible for creating the English kingdom was being linked from north to south with a deliberately selected set of saints, whose influence cut across ancient kingdom after kingdom. To those who did not know of the real pain and the real struggles at Athelney, a future was being magically carved by apparitions and fantasy. Some sense was being made out of this twilight world, in which the real Alfred

The Life of St Neot

Neot (d. *c.* 877) was an obscure character. He seems to have been a warrior who later renounced his lifestyle for life in a monastery. He was a sacristan at Glastonbury Abbey but later lived in Cornwall, at first alone, then with a growing group of other monks near Bodmin Moor. He was remembered (and given the status of a saint) because of his good work in caring for the poor. The Cornish village of St Neot and the Cambridgeshire town of St Neots are named after him. Whoever St Neot really was, it is in his Life written in the tenth century that we hear of the famous episodes during Alfred's time in the winter fastnesses of Somerset, principal amongst which is the famous story of the burning of the cakes and his subsequent chastisement by a swineherd's wife. By the time of the writing of the Life it was becoming clear that communities such as that at St Neots in Cambridgeshire could benefit from the inclusion in the tales of their own saint the legends of a real man, a figure whose influence crossed the boundaries of Cornish, West Saxon and Mercian spheres of influence.

lived. But is there anything in any of these tales to resemble some degree of actuality?

Alfred certainly will have done a lot of navel-gazing during his time at Athelney. But if we are to believe the *Life of St Neot* and the account of the always entertaining William of Malmesbury, then the practical considerations of military reconnaissance were also part and parcel of Alfred's fight back. While at Athelney, Alfred is supposed to have executed an operation in which he was dressed as a minstrel and infiltrated Guthrum's camp, along with another helper. They remained several days unrecognised and gathered a great deal of information before returning to Athelney. It has been the subject of many a beautiful painting, and although clearly fantastical in the sense that the king is most unlikely to have risked himself in the enterprise, the story would make sense if the covert operation had been carried out by men on his behalf, perhaps by those of Æthelnoth, whose stealth and loyalty have already been noted.

The Summoning

Alfred was going to need more than Æthelnoth if he was to overcome Guthrum by force of arms. Whatever he had learned from intelligence gained through infiltration seems to have been enough to have given the king cause for optimism. Perhaps he had learned that his presence in the misty Somerset landscape had troubled his enemy. Talk of the bandit who was once a king may have spread around the tables at Chippenham, the evidence only too plain in the nervous faces of those who had encountered Alfred's men while out in the countryside. The usurper of Chippenham may have had a hold on the kingdom, but how long would it last with Alfred still at large? Perhaps that hold was not as secure now as it was when the king had been hurled into the winter wasteland . . .

It was time now for Alfred to test whether he really had any support left in the countryside: enough that is, to win him back his kingdom. With the men of Somerset already at his side, thanks to Æthelnoth, Alfred sent messengers across his kingdom and summoned his fyrd. How many of them would answer his call, only time would tell. The Christmas desertion of many leading men made the outcome of this task a very difficult one to predict. If he could not summon the number he required now, he would never do so. Moreover, if his attempt to wrest the throne from Guthrum's sponsorship failed, the consequences for Alfred would be terminal. But somewhere, in what was left of Alfred's Wessex, lay 3,000–4,000 men who would still answer his call at any cost.

Across the heart of Dorset there grew a famous old forest known as Selwood. According to Asser, at its eastern end was a place known as Egbert's Stone. This was to be the meeting place: a place where Alfred's followers were summoned to gather at a prescribed time eight weeks after Easter; a place where Alfred would wait with bated breath, to see who would answer his call to arms. Nobody knows the details of the message sent out to the men of Wiltshire or that part of Hampshire the *Anglo-Saxon Chronicle* states 'was on this side of the sea'. This statement is taken to indicate either that part of the shire on the western side of Southampton Water, or those who had not sailed to Francia. The words of the messengers, however, will surely have been stirring ones – perhaps something akin to: *Your lord the king is still very much alive*

King Alfred's Tower

In 1762 Henry Hoare (1705–1780), a banker whose estate at Stourhead in Wiltshire was close to the spot claimed for Egbert's Stone, conceived an idea to build a red-brick tower and name it King Alfred's Tower. Hoare commissioned Henry Flitcroft, a Palladian-influenced architect to build the tower. It still stands to a height of 160ft, commanding imposing views of Alfred's kingdom. The tower was built to celebrate the ending of the seven years' war against France and the accession of George III, but being deliberately placed near Egbert's Stone, it was also on the ancient boundaries of the counties of Somerset, Dorset and Wiltshire and the tower had one corner of its triangular footprint in each county. The building was finished in 1772 and was completed at an estimated cost of between £5,000 and £6,000. It stands on a green sandstone plinth about 1 metre above ground level and is constructed of over 1.2 million red bricks forming walls 2 foot 9 inches thick, the walls being set in the Flemish Bond style and evidently there was no use of scaffolding throughout the project, with the workmen simply sitting on the structure as it rose. Modern visitors to the monument are frequently surprised to discover that the tower is completely hollow inside, having only a 205 step spiral staircase to lead the visitor on an exhausting climb to a viewing gallery which rewards him with views over three counties and the ancient trackway known as the Hardway.

The Viking Wars of Alfred the Great

and intends to win his kingdom at the sword's edge. If you trust in God you will bring those who owe you service to answer the call of the king at Egbert's Stone on the given day and when battle is won, you will be taken once again fondly into his heart . . . we can permit ourselves a little playful imagination here. This was a seminal moment in English history. Would the recipients of this message be puzzled, joyful or fearful?

The spring of 878 saw Alfred and his band prepare to emerge from the forest. As they did so, they could not have known they were writing a defining chapter in the history of a kingdom that would become the heartland of the nation of England. At Egbert's Stone there would indeed be a gathering large enough to prove that, even in exile, the House of Ecgberht of Wessex, through the last surviving son of Æthelwulf, could not be defeated by any pretender. The bonds of lordship that tied the remaining men of Wessex to Alfred were considerable. And much to his joy, so were the numbers of men who still abided by them.

It was on or around 4 May when Alfred waited at Egbert's Stone. His heart must have leapt when scouts reported the snake-like columns of warriors from Hampshire and Wiltshire, writhing their way through the trees towards him. Real or imagined, the prophecy of St Cuthbert had come true. The king would have his helpers. It is hardly surprising that Asser spills forth about it in the way he does:

> When they saw the king, receiving him (not surprisingly) as if one restored to life after suffering such great tribulations, they were filled with immense joy. They made camp there for one night. At the break of the following dawn the king struck camp and came to a place called Iley and made camp for one night.

What nights these must have been, full of happiness and trepidation. Much talk around the campfires will have focused on the struggle ahead. Was it possible that the beast of Chippenham could himself be hunted?

878 Edington

The Battle of Edington, May 878

Alfred's march to Iley had been made for a good reason. Many years before, and for hundreds of years afterwards, 'Iglea' in Eastleigh Wood, in Sutton Veny, had been the meeting place of the hundred courts of Heytesbury and Warminster. Here, at a well-known gathering point, Alfred might have expected to further swell his ranks with men from the country. It is clear that by now the news of Alfred's great undertaking had reached Guthrum at Chippenham. The Dane could hardly defend a newly acquired kingdom by choosing to withstand a siege at Chippenham, for he knew that kingdoms were not defended that way. So, as a ruler with followers to impress and an enemy to eliminate, he chose a positive course of action, and striking out across country, headed straight for Alfred.

If Alfred already knew how high the stakes were, then so too did Guthrum. Whoever won the forthcoming battle would win Wessex outright. The Dane had let Alfred go once before, but now had a chance to truly rid himself of the last human obstacle in the way of a great dream. The Danes therefore moved out from Chippenham to Bratton Camp, an Iron Age Hill fort, the ancient ramparts of which still offered some protection, as it sat now only a small distance from Alfred's force at Iley. Beneath Guthrum, at the lower end of the escarpment at the western limits of Salisbury Plain, was a small settlement known as Edington, a royal vill that Alfred gave to his queen.

Alfred, whose intentions seem to have been to march on Chippenham, could not reach that place without passing the old hill fort. Guthrum had therefore blocked his path. So, just 6 miles to the north-east of Iley, after striking camp at sunrise that morning, Alfred's scouts saw the Danish army forming up against the silhouette of rising banks of grass and wood, echoing an age of struggles long gone. The victor of this new confrontation at Edington would usher in a brand-new age in the history of the British Isles.

Alfred probably now moved his army to the high ground at Battlesbury, where yet another Iron Age Hillfort provided him with a vantage point and protection. From here he would launch a direct assault on the enemy in his path. Some chroniclers' accounts of the ensuing battle are coloured by flowery language, which describe the 'rampart' Alfred himself provided for his troops, simply by being a stalwart fighter. The king's presence is likened to that of an angel and his threefold armoury of faith, hope and the love of God are given more credence than the sequence of military events, which quickly got lost in the aftermath of the struggle. We are almost helpless on the matter, but we can deduce something about it.

Carrying on from the passage where Alfred and his men had settled at Iley for one night, Asser recalls the battle in limited

Anglo-Saxon Tactics

Anglo-Saxon warfare was largely an infantry affair, although evidence for the widespread usage of horses is now pointing to the adoption of mounted infantry as a strategic option in the years after Edington.

An English army of this period would square up to its enemy by ushering its horses to the rear and would form up in the famous shield wall formation with interlocking shields. With spears and sidearms at the ready the Anglo-Saxons would step forwards into battle crashing their shields against their weapons and exhorting their God.

There was no widespread deployment of the bow and arrow on the field of battle. This weapon was considered that of the poacher and not a weapon with which a man could prove his bravery. A warrior's prowess depended upon whether he was brave on the battlefield. Hand-to-hand combat was never an area in which the English armies of the day were found to be wanting. Traditionally, it is said that what the Anglo-Saxons lacked in tactical capability was made up for by an iron resolution. So long as the ground was conducive to a steamroller-like defence or attack, the Anglo-Saxon armies would win their battles. The problem came only when they were outwitted in the landscape.

detail, presumably mindful of the significance of the timing of the assault on Guthrum. It was Whitsun. Fifty days had passed since Alfred had been thrown into the winter wilderness. Whitsun commemorates the Holy Ghost's appearance before the apostles to show that Christ had risen from the dead. Here, on a muddy misty slope, as he peered before him, Guthrum saw a vision of a man surrounded by his die-hard followers, an embodiment of the Christian Faith, a seemingly invincible symbol of all the things he was not. In the absence of a proper description of the battle we can permit ourselves to believe, so strong is the evidence, that faith and fate did indeed win the day for Alfred and his men. Here, for what it is worth, is Asser's account:

> When the morning dawned, he moved his forces and came to a place called Edington, and fighting fiercely with a compact shield wall against the entire Viking army, he persevered resolutely for a long time; at length he gained the victory through God's will. He destroyed the Vikings with great slaughter, and pursued those who fled as far as the stronghold [probably Chippenham as opposed to Bratton Camp], hacking them down; he seized everything he found outside the stronghold – men (whom he killed immediately), horses and cattle – and boldly made camp in front of the gates of the Viking stronghold with all his army.

Like the other great battles in Anglo-Saxon history, Edington seems to have lasted a considerable time. Brunanburh (937) and Hastings (1066) also raged for the better part of the day. This is because, in these pitched battles, there had to be a resolution one way or the other. A profound defeat or the death of a leader would be the only acceptable reason for ending the struggle. Clearly, at Edington the stakes were high when the shield walls crashed into one another that day. We are told by Asser, however, some additional information not recorded elsewhere. The flight of any army from the battlefield is usually the time when the most casualties are sustained.

The Viking Wars of Alfred the Great

While the *Anglo-Saxon Chronicle* does not say what Alfred did when he got to the stronghold after the battle, it does mention that the English rode there. The existence of an Anglo-Saxon cavalry (by which we mean a dedicated horseback fighting unit) at the time of Alfred the Great is a subject historians squabble over. At Edington, as was hinted in the accounts of Ashdown, it seems a mounted reserve was used to chase down the enemy as it fled. To a military historian, such tactics smack of the use of mounted infantry fighting from horseback. To those who saw it with their own eyes, it must have looked just like cavalry.

Perhaps more importantly than the manner in which Alfred's men got to the stronghold, is what they were ordered to do when

Swords

The swords of the Alfredian period contrast greatly with those of the earlier age. During the first invasions of the Saxons into Britain in the fifth and sixth centuries, the swords used by the invaders were double-edged parallel or near parallel sided weapons which were 'point heavy', cumbersome and used to slash more than to fence. Over time, as the Anglo-Saxons took on a more defensive posture, the blades of swords became more tapering, thus pushing the point of balance back towards the hilt and making the weapon sit up in the hand of the user. This was good for flexibility. The swords of Alfred's day were characterised by strongly curving upper and lower pommel guards, curving away from the grip. Danish swords are thought to have displayed a tea cosy or D-shaped pommel.

The sword was a prized weapon, cherished from generation to generation. King Alfred himself left a sword in his will valued at 3,600 silver pennies. Ownership of such an item marked a man out as of noble bearing. The spear however, most likely remained the most widely employed weapon on the battlefield.

Spears

The principal weapon amongst the Anglo-Saxon warriors was the spear. It was the universal symbol of the free man wielded by all ranks in the army. If the sources are anything to go by, spears fall into a number of categories. These are listed below with their number of occurrences in Old English literature where known:

Aesc (25 times)

Gar (78 times)

Aetgar (14 times)

Aescberend (Spear bearer)

Aescthrace (Spearthwack!)

Daroð (dart)

Ord (spear tip)

Scutel (dart)

Spere (spear)

Gafeluc (a later form for Gar)

The Aesc was a prize weapon. It was named after its haft which was most often made of the springy and forgiving yet sturdy wood of the ash tree. There are accounts of these weapons being retained two handed in their owner's possession and being used on the battlefield in a thrusting and parrying manner. Nobody ever threw his Aesc away. They are often mentioned as being in the hands of veterans, heroes and noblemen.

The gar, or spear was a smaller weapon than the Aesc with a lighter iron blade and shorter haft. The gar is often described as a weapon in flight and it is clearly not a weapon used solely for thrusting and parrying.

Further down the list are the weapons which were not retained in the hands and which were thrown at close quarters on the battlefield. Into this category fall the daroð, the scutel and the gafeluc, a later term for the gar.

they got there. We must imagine Alfred's mindset at this time. The last surviving son of Æthelwulf had been exiled in his own kingdom, betrayed and forsaken by those who were prepared to side with the devil. With a small band of loyal followers he had survived by robbing his own people in the countryside as well as attacking his enemy. The indignity must have been over-whelming. Having managed to pull an army together through strength of personality, as reflected through the extent of powerful lordship ties, Alfred finally faced his enemy at Edington. The victory was certainly sweet, but the pursuit to Chippenham was deadly. Stragglers were killed, animals seized outside the gates. Somewhere in the middle of the retreating throng of exhausted warriors was a fearful Guthrum. The Danes' ability to withstand a siege was neutralised within a few hours. This is a side of Alfred we hear little about. He was clearly a resolute warrior when he needed to be. As for his ability to show mercy, it came with terms that made any subsequent agreement one-sided to say the least. Alfred, king of Wessex, had returned to take his kingdom from the heathens. Nothing in English history would ever be quite the same again.

Baptism at Aller

Had he fought anything like a king, Guthrum would have fallen on the field at Edington that day. By seeking safety with his comrades behind the gates of Chippenham, Guthrum had thrown away his cause. The dream was over. The lying and the treachery had led ultimately to nothing, and both he and Alfred knew it. Alfred would later write how he viewed those who broke their oaths. To Alfred, who had suffered at the hands of dishonest enemies for so long, the binding of an oath was of paramount importance. It was the glue that held Anglo-Saxon politics together. But the man behind the gates at Chippenham had shown himself to be no heeder of the Anglo-Saxon custom. And so Alfred sent no one in to negotiate with him, he just sat there, triumphant, and waited.

Conditions inside the camp must have been awful. The psychological impact of a crushing defeat at the hands of a seemingly immortal man would have been compounded by what Guthrum saw around him. People were dying of their wounds, from disease, or starving from lack of food. The siege went on day after day, and the resolve of the Danes grew weaker. Alfred knew he had his prey where he wanted him. Sooner or later, Guthrum would have to accept defeat and come out. It happened a full two weeks after the siege began.

There would be no negotiation, no exchange of hostages, no bargains and no oaths, bar one, which might be broken. Nor would any money be paid to Guthrum. The heathens were shattered. When the Danish embassy crept from the gates towards the Anglo-Saxon camp, he brought a message of abject surrender. Now, two weeks into a siege that had brought the required results, the king decided to show mercy. He could easily have slaughtered the Danes, but instead chose the following course. The king would take as many chosen hostages as he liked from the Danish ranks and expect no demand for hostages on their part. And so it was arranged. Out came the chosen hostages unarmed and helpless. The one oath that was sworn was the obvious one: the rest of the army would leave Alfred's kingdom at once.

But how, in the light of countless broken agreements in the past, does a Christian king make a heathen leader stick to his promise to leave? We might recall that at Wareham Alfred had tried with limited success to get the enemy to agree to terms by swearing not on Christian relics but on their own sacred ring, something they had not done hitherto. Now, with all the cards in his hands, Alfred was in a position to try something that had been successful to a degree on the Continent and had often been practised in Anglo-Saxon England to express symbolically one ruler's superiority over another. Guthrum must have found it an easy decision to accept being baptised into the Christian faith. We might allow ourselves to believe that he intended to revert to his old ways once he was out of the corner he had got himself into. But there were the hostages to think about. We do not know their names or their relationship to Guthrum, but we can be sure that Alfred chose them carefully and that, unlike previous hostage-giving episodes, the Dane could not callously disregard them.

The Viking Wars of Alfred the Great

Alfred was now a forward thinker. Guthrum would be of more use to him as a living Christian friend than a dead pagan enemy. Three nervous weeks went by before Guthrum and thirty of his best men were led by the English through the fastnesses of the Somerset Levels, where they had themselves once roamed in exile. To the small church at Aller they came. The ceremony of turning a pagan into a Christian left nothing to chance. The thirty men, dressed in white robes, entered the small church to renounce their allegiance to Odin publicly. Even before they entered, a priest blew into their faces to exorcise the evil spirits that had so dominated their actions in the past. This paved the way for the full ceremony to take place. Each man was signed with the cross in numerous places before having salt placed in their mouths (symbolising the food of divine wisdom) and then immersed in holy water to represent the cleansing of the spirit. As Guthrum plunged into the holy water he was dragged back out as a Christian man. The man whose hand was responsible for bringing this hardened northern warrior into the Anglo-Saxon world was Alfred himself. When it came to the actual baptism, Guthrum was required to ask formally for it to take place and his head was anointed with a chrism and a white fillet was bound to the spot where the anointing had taken place, not to be removed for another eight days. Guthrum was no longer a pagan warrior with a strange sounding barbaric name, but emerged from the church at Aller as Athelstan, King Alfred's godson.

Guthrum had been given a name synonymous with the royal line of the House of Ecgberht. There were Athelstans before him and there would be a powerful Athelstan in the next century, one of the most powerful men in English history. None of these men held rank lower than ætheling. And so Guthrum left Aller to partake in celebrations, which preceded his chrism loosening at nearby Wedmore eight days later. Now he was a king, able to plan his future outside Wessex, and able to call on his godfather should he need him. How long it would all last, only time would tell. Significantly, when it came to the chrism-loosening ceremony at Wedmore, Guthrum was purified by Æthelnoth, Alfred's most loyal subject, who had stood by him during the toughest times. The symbolism was complete. The House of Ecgberht had not only survived, it was now contemplating possibilities that, until now, had been unthinkable.

A King Restored

For twelve days Alfred and Guthrum spent their time engaging in feasting and gift-giving. Guthrum received from Alfred a great many treasures, as did many of his men. It was a form of welcome into the Christian world of Anglo-Saxon Wessex, couched in old-style pagan exchanges the Danes would have understood well. In this ninth-century world of overt symbolism, Alfred was demonstrating the superiority of his position as a great gift-giver.

Alfred was now just into his thirties. He was in his prime. He had behind him a following that believed in him more now than ever before, such was the significance of events at Edington, Aller and Wedmore. A dangerous enemy had been pacified and converted, and the old voices of dissent were stifled, for the time being, soon to be removed by the king entirely. But Alfred knew that the future was far from certain. Would Guthrum, as the new Athelstan, be able to keep his side of the bargain when he left Chippenham? Had Alfred really done enough to secure his kingdom from treachery and deceit? Above all, there was another pressing concern on his mind. As the king's scouts observed the heels of the Danish army trotting back to Chippenham, Alfred was already formulating a grand defensive plan to change the way in which the English defended themselves. It would take all the organisational capabilities available in Alfred's kingdom. He would draw upon what he had seen on his own travels to France and to Rome. The wars of attrition that had resulted in the Danes and the Anglo-Saxons fighting each other to a virtual standstill were over. The resulting scheme of a grand defence-in-depth network of fortifications, each with assigned garrisons has left an indelible mark on the southern English towns and countryside to this day, and is evidence of, perhaps, the first great exercise in English military engineering. This king would not lose his kingdom twice.

The Viking Wars of Alfred the Great

Quite why Guthrum did not move out of Chippenham until October 878 is a mystery. It is a period of activity we know little about. Guthrum chose to move his force to Cirencester that year and it spent the winter in this symbolic place, with tents set within the remains of what was once a splendid Roman town, and which no doubt retained some semblance of its former glory. Now, it was situated in the southern part of the land of the Hwicce, an ancient English subkingdom of Mercia. Perhaps this was an ideal place from which to observe the politics of both Wessex and Mercia, and perhaps even for Guthrum to receive news of any Welsh activity across the border.

During this period of apparent calm, both Alfred and Guthrum were waiting for something to happen. Ceolwulf II was ill. Should he die, which one of them would be able to seize the opportunity to bring Mercia under their sway? The year of 879 was the turning point for the future of an entire country. A vision was forming in the mind of Alfred, a vision of an expanded kingdom, incorporating the English half of Mercia along with Wessex. But before this vision could be realised, Alfred would have to lay the foundations through the usual tool of medieval statecraft. Before we see how this was done, we must turn to two significant events in 879, which helped pave the way for Alfred's plan.

They were almost certainly the remnants of the Viking force defeated by Carloman and Louis III of Francia who sailed up the River Thames and anchored at Fulham outside London. They found for themselves an old Roman fortification, which, although small, they reused. Their presence would surely have worried King Alfred, as their location controlled the old Roman road of Akeman Street, which led west into the heart of Wessex and which crossed the Thames at Staines.

But what was Guthrum's role in all this? It would seem that the Fulham force had come from their defeat in Francia into England to try their luck in a new land, in much the same way as many Viking forces had in the past hopped around western Europe, shifting from place to place, as the going got tough for them. Asser gives us a puzzling account of the presence of the new threat on the northern borders of Wessex and suggests that 'they made contact with the army further upstream'. However, the subsequent move of Guthrum, who took his entire force to East Anglia and settled there as ruler, and the fact that Asser also tells us the Fulham force overwintered at Fulham and then left England for Ghent in Eastern Francia, suggests that, if the Fulham force and Guthrum's men were ever in league, then it has yet to show itself in the historical record. The possibility remains, however, that both these forces were still intent on hovering menacingly over Wessex for a while, until events turned against them.

The years that followed would be, by no means, peaceful for Alfred, but the dynamics of the campaigns were changing. There was a great deal of rebuilding to do across Alfred's kingdom, and it began almost immediately with the instigation of a burghal system of fortifications. These fortified places, positioned strategically in the landscape across the new kingdom, would provide the springboard for a remarkable recovery, and they heralded the arrival into the English theatre of a new kind of warfare. The battle of Edington truly marks the end of the old style of military provision for the kingdom of Wessex. From now on, one king would mastermind a military revival of Carolingian proportions in England, the effects of which would resound in hall and castle alike for centuries to come.

879–884 The Rebuilding

Laying the Foundations

Alfred was a changed man. Newly invigorated with what seemed to be boundless energy, he set about transforming his kingdom. Politically, the king undertook a long overdue purge of characters of dubious loyalty within his court, which had profound effects on the make-up of the witan. Those who had shown themselves to have been fickle in the recent wars, and those whose historical loyalties had not lain with Alfred but with other members of his extended family, were removed from government. Almost half of the old guard was replaced by the king. In their place came men who held lordship ties with Alfred and for whom that bond was strong. For so long Alfred had struggled to combat not just the dishonest Dane, but the turncoat Englishman. But now there would be no disloyalty. The veterans of Edington would help Alfred run his kingdom.

The question of Alfred's inheritance from his father and the agreement he had had with his brother Æthelred needed attention too. At a meeting held at Langdene, the king won, or rather coerced, the approval of the witan sometime in the early 880s to the effect that everything in his father's will should come to him, and that he should do with it as he pleased. This gave Alfred the greatest power of all – the power to reward his followers. Furthermore, it made the question of the succession clearer in the minds of the people. If anyone other than the son of the king claimed the throne they would have to have a good reason for it and enough of a following either inside or outside the kingdom to turn that claim into a tangible challenge. One day that challenge would come, but for now, Alfred and his issue were in the ascendancy.

With the Danes settled now in the eastern part of Mercia a new human geography had to be acknowledged. Here, Alfred would have to come to terms with Guthrum and accept that beyond the old Roman road known as Watling Street, things would be done very differently. This famous old road, which leads north-west out of London, effectively bisects the ancient kingdom of Mercia. To the north and east of this road lay a vast stretch of land that would in time become known as the *Danelaw*, on account of its acquired Scandinavian legal and social characteristics. Within a generation some of these settlers and their children would have to decide whether their loyalty lay with a southern English king or a great Norse warlord in the ferocious campaigns that stained the soil of northern Britain in the tenth century. Now, however, they were content to remain loyal to their Danish leaders.

On the English side of the divide, to the south of Watling Street, something remarkable had happened. Ceolwulf II had died and Alfred imposed himself and his kin into the political vacuum. There is a suggestion that the man who took control of the English half of Mercia in the early 880s was a relative of Alfred's father-in-law. This man, named Æthelred, would rule English Mercia not as a king, but as an ealdorman. He is known to have acknowledged Alfred as his overlord. He had not come from the dynasty of Ceolwulf and many of Ceolwulf's followers are not traceable after this period, indicating that Alfred was more than aware of the fractious state of English Mercian politics and was loath to watch history repeat itself. The transformation that was taking place in Alfred's expanded kingdom was acknowledged not just at home but abroad too. A letter to Alfred from the archbishop of Rheims, datable to the mid-880s, addressed the king as *Regi Anglorum*. This title was in contrast to those mentioned in the earlier charters of the 880s, which referred to Alfred as *Westseaxena cinge* or *Saxonum rex*. By the end of the decade, Alfred ruled the whole kingdom of the Anglo-Saxons. Soon, his son and grandson would create from this kingdom a still further expanded polity, the kingdom of the English. But first, there was a great project to complete.

Fortifying Wessex

> *If every hide is represented by one man, then every pole of wall can be manned by four men. Then for the maintenance of 20 poles of wall 80 hides are required and for a furlong, 160 hides are required by the same reckoning.*

How did Alfred manage to reconstruct his kingdom? Or as Asser puts it:

> And what of the cities and towns to be rebuilt and of others to be constructed where previously there were none?

English kings had, in the past, turned to fortification as a means of defence. King Offa of Mercia (757–796) had made fortification-building against the threat of the Vikings a part of the system of land tenure and military obligation, but nothing was undertaken on anything like the scale of Alfred's project. Alfred remembered his own experience at Nottingham, recalled also how the Dane had little stomach for a siege. Furthermore, having himself travelled widely, the king will have seen the coordinated papal urban defences of Pope Leo IV in Rome, and will have known of Charles the Bald's fortification programme instigated in the late 860s, which saw the defences of the towns of Angoulême, Tours, Le Mans and Dijon rebuilt according to a new defensive philosophy. Charles the Bald in 868 had also looked at the twin forts at Pont de l'Arche and realised after their capture by Vikings in 865–866 that a re-organisation of service duties was required, so he carefully divided the fortifications into sections, for which individual landowners would have the responsibility for manning and maintenance. Charles's great rebuilding exercise had involved a Domesday-like survey of the taxable land in his kingdom, and it is not inconceivable that before he commenced his work on his own kingdom, Alfred undertook a similar survey.

An idea began to form in Alfred's mind. Alfred was keen not only to provide protection for his people should there be any further Danish incursions, but also to provide a system of military provision that he could rely on all year round. What happened in the landscape of southern England in the 880s is testimony to the organisational genius of King Alfred. Not only was Alfred engaged in beseeching foreign archbishops for their finest scholars to help him rebuild the moral and intellectual fibre of his kingdom, the king set about a physical restructuring on a grand strategic scale. That the great rebuilding of towns and cities in the south of England took place is evidenced by later testimony from William of Malmesbury, who, writing in the twelfth century, stated that he had seen with his own eyes an inscription in the chapter house at Shaftesbury, stating that 'Alfred Made This Town in 880'. This remarkable piece of historical evidence was given further credence when, in 1902, a fragment of what was surely the very same inscription was discovered. One can imagine similar inscriptions at each of the burhs in the system. Alfred was sending a message to his people and in doing so was taking pride in his new industriousness.

Listed in a document known as the Burghal Hidage, a sixteenth-century transcript of an eleventh-century Winchester document, are thirty-three strongholds accompanied by a note of how many hides of land are attributable to each place. Cornwall, Kent and London are missing from the list, possibly because at the time of its original compilation, these areas were under semi-independent jurisdiction, like Kent and Cornwall, or controlled from English Mercia, like London. However, while Exeter, Bath, Winchester, Portchester, Chichester, Rochester and Canterbury form an obvious network of key strongholds, those in Kent are missing from the record. It has been argued that Alfred's refortification programme had not yet pushed as far east as central and eastern Kent on the eve of the return of the Danes to England in 892. This might explain why, when they came, the Danes chose Kent in which to land. The king seems to have removed animals and supplies from the land in Kent before the return of the Danes, and this might explain why the enemy came back to England so laden with horses and supplies. But at what stage the Kentish areas were properly fortified along the lines of the rest of Wessex remains a mystery.

The surviving list of fortifications shows that the burhs were not merely situated on the frontiers of the kingdom, but were carefully placed within the kingdom so that no burh would be more than a day's march from another, a distance generally taken to be about 20 miles. The defences worked not only as places of refuge for the local population during times of Danish incursion, but as bases from which to dominate a territory under hostile attack. The strongholds were close enough together for each of the garrisons to support each other in the event of combined military action. The estimated garrison strength of all the burhs of Wessex was around 27,000 men. Not all of them would take to the field at any one time, but the sheer numbers meant that wherever an enemy went inside Wessex, he would not be far from hostile opposition.

Alfred made just as much use of the old Roman walled cities

as he did of building new burhs in the Wessex landscape. The guiding principle was the distance that separated each of the forts. Not every fort went on to become a town in later years, but the refortification of the larger places provided the springboard for what would become a gradual urbanisation during the tenth century. Mercantile activity, coin production and legal jurisdiction became key functions of many of these places in the decades to come. So, as the burgesses moved into the new towns, as the prices for burghal plots rose, a new economy formed. Alfred had brought urban life back to the south of England for the first time since the Roman era and had created a new class of industrious and businesslike officials, whose later namesakes would play a vital role in the economic life of medieval England.

But it did not happen overnight. To rebuild a kingdom takes years. As we shall observe, as late as 892 one small fort in Kent was still being built by only a handful of men when it was descended upon by the enemy. It was not that people in Alfred's kingdom were unused to having to perform the duties popularly known as the 'Common Burdens'. They had been part of the social fabric for some time. These 'burdens' were bridgework, fortress-building and military service. Asser, however, in one important passage of his biography, gives us a glimpse of the difficulties Alfred faced in getting people to understand the importance of the work they were undertaking. This insight into the agonies of Anglo-Saxon kingship has a refreshing personal angle to it, when we bear in mind that, according to Asser at least, Alfred the Great ruled with a mind half distracted by illness:

> King Alfred has been transfixed by the nails of many tribulations, even though he is invested with royal authority [. . .] he has been plagued continually with the savage attacks of some unknown disease, such that he does not have even a single hour of peace in which he does not suffer from the disease itself or else, gloomily dreading it, is not driven almost to despair [. . .] And what of the mighty disorder and confusion of his own

people – to say nothing of his own malady – who would undertake of their own accord little or no work for the common needs of the kingdom?

Yet once he had taken over the helm of his kingdom, he alone, sustained by divine assistance, struggled like an excellent pilot to guide his ship [. . .] For by gently instructing, cajoling, urging, commanding and (in the end when his patience was exhausted) by sharply chastising those who were disobedient and by despising popular stupidity and stubbornness in every way, he carefully and cleverly exploited and converted his bishops and ealdormen and nobles, and his thegns most dear to him, and reeves as well (in all of whom, after the Lord and the king, the authority of the entire kingdom is seen to be invested, as is appropriate), to his own will and to the general advantage of the whole realm. But if, during the course of these royal admonitions, the commands were not fulfilled because of the people's laziness, or else (having been begun too late in a time of necessity) were not finished in time to be of use to those working on them (I am speaking here of fortifications commanded by the king which have not yet been begun, or else, having been begun late in the day, have not been brought to completion) and enemy forces burst in by land and sea (or, as frequently happens, by both!), then those who had opposed the royal commands were humiliated in meaningless repentance by being reduced to virtual extinction [. . .] Those who were severely afflicted, therefore, are contrite in untimely repentance, and are sorry that they had negligently scorned the royal commands; now they loudly applaud the king's foresight and promise to make every effort to do what they had previously refused – that is, with respect to constructing fortresses and to the other things of general advantage to the whole kingdom.

Soon, the efforts of the king and his weary people would be tested. The system would be pushed to the limit perhaps only halfway through its construction. But the cities and forts were only part of the great Alfredian reforms. The king had also been paying attention to two other aspects of his military capabilities, both on land and at sea.

Military Reforms

There is good evidence to suggest that, as well as building new fortifications and garrisoning them, the king divided the labour of his land forces into three parts. The *Anglo-Saxon Chronicle* states, in an entry for 893, almost by way of a reminder to its reader, that

> The king had separated his army into two so that there was always half at home and half out except for those men who had to hold the fortresses.

It is thought that this division was made long before the system was tested in the 890s and that it has its origin in the reforms of the 880s. But what does it mean? To some, this statement smacks of Orosius's account of the Amazon army splitting into two parts, one to go out and fight and the other to defend their homes. The statement may in part be an oblique reference to Orosius, but in reality the rotation system really was put into action on the ground. It meant that for each man serving with the king in the field there was one other man tending to the land, which supported that warrior and another man on the wall of a fort. Each division of service was allocated for a set period and the one group would take over the duties of the other when that time arose. It effectively indicated that the kingdom would, from now on, always be in a state of readiness for the arrival of an enemy. In reality, there were complications with the system, particularly when one relief failed to replace another when the time came for it to return home, but it was a better arrangement than anything that had gone before.

The Danes more often than not attacked their victims' coastlines in combined operations, as Asser knew only too well, their shallow-draft vessels could penetrate inland and travel far up the river systems. It was clear to Alfred that he needed a naval deterrent. His brother Athelstan had fought a sea engagement against a Viking fleet off the coast of Kent and there had been other notable victories in the past, not least the encounter Alfred himself had in 875, which resulted in the capture of one of the enemy vessels. It is in the post-Edington era that Alfred paid attention to his navy. Asser hints that the later fleet of the 890s was 'Alfred's Fleet', indicating that this was in effect a 'Royal Navy'. It is supposed to be a much-loved Victorian myth that Alfred was the founder of the Royal Navy, but it remains the case that from Alfred's time to our own there has always been a naval force in England directly associated with the reigning English monarch, and it seems churlish to deprive Alfred of the accolade. Throughout the ports and shipyards of southern England the work began. The enemy would have one of their main advantages challenged in the future – their power to dominate the sea.

The Vikings in France

The Viking force that came to Fulham in the winter of 878–879 left for France, allowing Alfred to lick his wounds and commence the grand rebuilding of his kingdom. The *Anglo-Saxon Chronicle* and Æthelweard, who was working from a now lost copy of the same, both take a keen interest in events across the water in the early years of the 880s. It is quite probable that this obsession with the movements of pagan forces in foreign lands, as recorded in the *Chronicle*, represents the influx into Alfred's kingdom of Continental scholars and clerics, who were themselves all part of the rebuilding programme.

It may have been news from the Continent, combined with their hearing of recent Danish catastrophes in England, which persuaded the Fulham force to try their luck again in the land of the Franks. And so to Ghent they came. Charles the Fat (839–888), the new Holy Roman Emperor, was the target for Danish aggression. Already harassed by a force at Asselt, headed by a Viking chieftain named Godafrid, Charles's problems had only just begun. He had managed successfully to besiege Godafrid, but the terms of the subsequent negotiations were incomparable to those agreed by Alfred and Guthrum.

The Viking Wars of Alfred the Great

Charles handed over 2,412 pounds of purest gold and silver, gave lands to Godafrid in return for his acknowledgement as Godafrid's overlord, and then, to make matters worse, withdrew his forces 6 miles to allow Godafrid room for manoeuvre. The contrast with Alfred could not be stronger. Godafrid went on to laugh in the face of the Holy Roman Emperor by seizing, killing or ransoming the noble visitors Charles had sent him.

If the kingdom of the Anglo-Saxons was filled with the noise of hammers, saws and chisels that year, then for the Continental realms it was quite different. The sounds of swords on shields, the smell of death and burning everywhere prevailed. The Emperor had to rob his churches to pay off various Viking leaders, causing resentment throughout the land. Bishops themselves took up arms and launched themselves in forlorn attacks on the formidable enemy. If they could not fight, they ran. Bishop Hincmar of Rheims found himself without the protection of the local nobility, who were away with the emperor, so he fled laden with saintly relics, treasures and the very annals in which he recorded the disaster. These annals, the *Annals of St Bertin*, were soon to be written in another hand, as Hincmar was nearing death. But here in these last few lines of his work, Hincmar mentioned a Viking leader who would soon come to test Alfred's new defences. Hæsten had been active in the Loire Valley area but had recently been bribed by Louis III to go elsewhere. It is just possible that, on his way to the coastal strip between the Seine and Frisia, he teamed up with the force that had encamped at Fulham in 879.

The *Anglo-Saxon Chronicle*, the words of which are quoted below, while following the progress of the Vikings abroad between 881 and 884, also drops a hint or two that Alfred's shipmen were not idle during this time. The passage also outlines the wide-ranging contacts enjoyed by the king and his churchmen, even at a time of great national crisis:

881 Here the raiding army went further into the land of the Franks, and the Franks fought against them [at the battle of Saucourt on the Somme, 3 August 881], and

there the raiding army was provided with horses after the fight.

882 [881] Here the raiding army went up along the Meuse further into the land of the Franks and settled there for a year [Æthelweard says they laid out a camp at Elsloo on the river Maas]. And the same year [882] King Alfred went out to sea with ships and fought against 4 shiploads of Danishmen and took two of the ships, and killed the men; and two surrendered to him and the men were badly knocked around and wounded before they surrendered.

883 Here the raiding army went up the Scheldt to Condé [to a monastery of Nuns, according to Asser] and settled there for a year. And Pope Marinus sent the wood of the Lord to King Alfred and the same year Sigehelm and Athelstan took to Rome – and also to St Thomas in India [possibly Judea] and to St Bartholemew – the alms which King Alfred had vowed to send there when they besieged the raiding army in London, and there, by the grace of God, they were very successful in obtaining their prayers in accordance with those vows.

884 [883] Here the raiding army went up the Somme to Amiens and settled there for a year.

The battle of Saucourt had indeed been a rare victory for the Franks and it was celebrated in a contemporary Old High German poem called *Ludwigslied*, and in the Old French *Gormond et Isembard*. The chronicler's assertion, however, that the Vikings were 'provided with horses after the fight' is more than backed up by Asser, who states that, once battle was over, the Vikings 'became a mounted force'. It would seem that the Vikings could gain items of strategic value even in defeat.

The Vikings left Ghent in November 880, having spent a year raiding up the Scheldt and further south in the region of Rheims. They spent the winter of 880–881 at Courtrai, on the River Lys, and from here they ravaged Flanders. By the summer they had crossed the Somme as far as Beauvais, before being checked by Louis III at Saucourt in August. By the autumn of that year, they had moved from Flanders into Lotharingia, settling for the winter at Elsloo. For the first part of 882 they devastated the area bounded by the rivers Meuse, Rhine and Moselle, eventually being besieged by Charles the Fat. After this, they turned west towards the Scheldt. Around this time King Alfred was tackling some of their compatriots at sea.

From their winter camp at Condé, the heathens raided to the south and south-west until the spring of 883, when their attention turned to ravaging the coast of Flanders until the autumn. They laid camp for the forthcoming winter at Amiens, where Carloman (866–884), Louis III's successor, tried in vain to sue for peace. By the autumn of 884 the force was in Boulogne, and it seems its leadership took a decision not unlike that taken by the Great Heathen Army at Repton: namely, to split up. For the inhabitants of Louvain, on the River Dyle, it would be more of the usual brutal treatment, but for the king of the Anglo-Saxons, it would be the first great test of his rebuilt kingdom. The Viking force, so successful in Francia, had chosen to sail across the Channel and try their luck in England. They came by ship to Rochester. They had brought their horses with them and expected to be able to conduct a fruitful campaign in the Kentish countryside.

Rochester, the First Test

Rochester must have seemed like the perfect target for the new arrivals. It was an important port with its own bishopric at the end of various lucrative cross-Channel trade routes. As far as the men who had been part of the Fulham force in 879 were concerned, they had no reason to suspect from their own observations of Alfred's kingdom that Rochester would be any better protected than it had been back in 842, when both it and London had been attacked with great loss to the English.

But what happened next showed the Danes that there had been a remarkable change in the south of England. When they landed at Rochester, they found it defended. The old walls were repaired and manned, and there was a garrison present, strong enough to laugh their attack to scorn. Immediately, the invading force had to opt for something its leadership had not planned. They dug themselves a fort at the entrance to the city. Perhaps they thought they could starve the inhabitants out. They were mistaken in many respects. The older veterans, who may well have campaigned in Wessex during the early part of the Viking wars, will have known how long it took for a traditional Anglo-Saxon army to muster in the countryside. They will have calculated that their besieging force would have had at least two weeks' grace before it could expect the army of the king to appear. But they had not accounted for the reforms Alfred had been instigating. The king of the Anglo-Saxons fell upon the besiegers outside the gates of Rochester using speed and surprise. The enemy was scattered and it panicked. People ran from their stronghold and left behind their prisoners and their horses, both of which they had brought over from Francia.

Asser tells us that, after the Danes were surprised, they sailed once again for Francia, forced by this 'unavoidable turn of events'. But Æthelweard gives us a valuable insight into what might have happened next. Only some of them sailed away, it seems. Those who stayed behind exchanged hostages with Alfred, but twice broke their agreement with the king and went raiding in the forested areas south of the Thames. Alfred, for a while, must have wondered what was giving these remaining Danes such confidence. When he discovered the answer to this puzzle he will not have been pleased at all. Guthrum and his men had been quiet since the great defeat at Edington, but now the canny Dane must have seen a chance to pile the pressure back onto Alfred. Æthelweard gives us an account, not given anywhere else, and he lets us know how he feels in recalling the treachery of the East Anglian Danes, at a time when they should have been tilling the fertile plains of the eastern kingdom, as opposed to meddling with Alfred's affairs once more:

The foul people who then held East Anglia gave support, and suddenly made an expedition outside their boundaries to Benfleet [in Essex]. There the allied force was divided by a grim quarrel, some remained, some sought places beyond the sea.

Guthrum's men had clearly not given up their passion for making trouble at Alfred's expense. Their effrontery was not to be tolerated. Alfred's fledgling navy was soon sent around the coast to East Anglia. The men of Kent, most probably from Rochester, set sail for the coast of Guthrum's kingdom with the intention of conducting a punitive campaign of ravaging, a sight so familiar to Viking eyes. But the Danes of East Anglia saw the English coming and confidently sailed out to meet them. Results would show there was no foundation for such confidence. Quite why the naval battle at the mouth of the River Stour went so well for the English will never be known. Of the sixteen Danish vessels that went out against the English king, none returned. All were captured and all of the men killed. It was a battle that must have shocked Guthrum, whose Danish manpower resources were reduced in one bloody day at the hands of a man who had now become his nemesis. But Guthrum was not so depleted after all. To the surprise of the English captains, who sat at anchor in the mouth of the Stour gloating over their booty, a fleet of Danish East Anglians came upon them just as they were beginning to head for Kent. They had come from everywhere in the East Anglian kingdom. Guthrum was flexing his muscles despite his recent setback. The ensuing Danish victory, although described nowhere in as much detail as the initial English victory, seems to have been no less profound. Almost certainly a great deal of the booty captured by Alfred's men in the original encounter was reclaimed by the Danes. Quite how many of Alfred's ships returned home is unclear.

But one thing was clear to the king of the Anglo-Saxons: Guthrum was not a spent force. A glance at a map of the political geography of southern and eastern England, at a time when the East Anglian Danes were still not content to put down their swords, showed one glaring problem. The town of London, for so long a Mercian trading port, was eminently vulnerable. This perfectly placed settlement, still only half occupied since Roman times, would form the focus of the next stage of the wars of Alfred the Great, and the way in which he dealt with the problem would have significant effects on the burgeoning sense of unity that his people were experiencing.

886 London

For hundreds of years the main Anglo-Saxon settlement at London lay beyond the old Roman walls to the west of the city. Inside the walls were still the crumbling remains of a once great seat of provincial Roman government. Outside, the traders of Lundenwic plied their trade on the sloping banks of the Thames, perhaps just a little afraid of the ghosts of the Roman past nearby. The area around Aldwych still bears the name that indicates its former role. We should not imagine that the London of this period was in anyway sparsely populated. If a person stood in the area of modern Covent Garden and looked to the south, he would see nothing but a hive of merchant activity centred on the numerous shallow-draft vessels pulled up onto the beaches of the Thames where the business of trading took place.

But times were changing. It may be the case that London was still an international centre of trade, much as the Venerable Bede had described it centuries earlier, but its inhabitants and visitors were in jeopardy. Just like their counterparts in the southern coastal trading ports, such as that at Hamwih near Southampton, the traders were susceptible to hit-and-run raids from the Viking adventurers. In reality, however, it seems that the Danes themselves had begun to understand the strategic importance of London, as opposed to extracting its portable wealth in raids. Ever since the partition of Mercia in 877, the kingdom that traditionally owned London, the settlement attracted Danish interest. It may well be that the force that sailed to Fulham chose to do so in order to exercise an influence over the place and prevent West Saxon access to it by river before it sailed off to foreign shores.

London was too big a prize for the Danes to miss. The agreement made between Alfred and Guthrum after Edington, in which Mercia was split in two, may well have left London to the English, but in reality it is likely that the Danish presence there was seen as something of an infestation. We are not sure how much historical information we are missing in the crucial years between 880 and 886. It is possible that London between these years was the crucible of a grand strategic struggle involving the Mercian ealdorman, the Danish leaders and Alfred himself. How many times it changed hands we do not know. The enigmatic statement of the chronicler that, in 883, Alfred sent alms to Rome, which the king 'had vowed to send there when they besieged the raiding army in London', may be a simple statement of truth. Furthermore, between 885 and 886 the settlement may well have attracted Danes from the allied force which had split up at Benfleet.

Whatever the real reason for Alfred's assault on London in 886, its effects were tremendous. The chronicler celebrates the taking of London by saying that 'all the English race' turned to Alfred 'except what was in captivity to Danish men; and he entrusted the fort to Ealdorman Æthelred to hold'. So, while arranging for the town to be handed over to a loyal pair of English hands, Alfred set about a wholesale rebuilding of the city of London. Danes would no longer hide away in the ruins of the old Roman town. The new burh of London would be planted right over the top of the old city and the settlement at Lundenwic would be abandoned in favour of a new policy of ensuring that trade took place inside the new burh. Markets would be set up within the walls. A street system was planned out in the town, the boundaries of which were now 1,100 yards from east to west and around 330 yards from north to south. But Alfred will have remembered that the Fulham force had sailed beyond London to Fulham and effectively blocked river traffic coming upstream to London from inland. To prevent this from ever happening again, Alfred constructed a second burh on the south side of the Thames. This was to be built by the men of Surrey and became known as the Suddringa Geworc, or in its modern sense, Southwark. The organisational complexities surrounding this fortress-building in the London area must have been on a Carolingian scale. Alfred clearly was borrowing ideas from Charles the Bald in his approach to solving the problem of the defence of the new London.

886 London

But what of Guthrum and of the English power base in west Mercia? Here, Alfred turned to a masterful piece of statecraft. Where would Alfred's new London fit into the king's grand strategy? There is no doubt that the new-look London was an Alfredian concept, built along the same lines as so many other southern fortified towns. But Alfred was a political animal. When it came to the handing out of land along the waterfront, where there were to be lucrative wharves, he gave one allotment to Æthelred of Mercia. This area, once known to Anglo-Saxons as *Æthelredes Hyd* became known later in the twelfth century as Queenhithe, taking its name from Queen Matilda. There is a reason for all this generosity towards the Mercian ealdorman. Alfred's daughter, Æthelflæd, was given in marriage to Æthelred. With her, came the gift of London, planted firmly back into the hands of its rightful owner. Alfred could be sure that his own interests in London would be presided over by his daughter. In the generation that followed, the woman who became known as 'the Lady of the Mercians' did perhaps more than even her royal father to fashion an English identity in the Danish-influenced north. Her military campaigns of the tenth century would see her command from the saddle and push the limits of English Mercian power to the very borders of Northumbria, where they had once been so many years ago. What we know of this formidable woman in her later years, gives us a clue as to why Alfred chose her for the role of a Mercian princess. Æthelflæd, like her father, was a born leader.

So, with London held in the name of the king of the Anglo-Saxons by a Mercian lord, Alfred turned to consolidate the agreement he had made with Guthrum in the aftermath of Edington. Some time had passed since that fateful battle, and with London now firmly in the hands of the Anglo-Saxons, the agreement needed revisiting.

The Treaty of Wedmore Revisited

A copy of a document survives from the eleventh century, supposedly referring to the era immediately after the capture of London, which defines the boundaries between English and

The Viking Wars of Alfred the Great

Danish areas of influence. It is a famous historical document, over which historians have argued for centuries. It is possible that, in its twisted and tortured boundary descriptions, particularly in the areas to the north and east of London, there is hidden a history of the two sides jockeying for position during the years 880–886. This may well be the case, but the text of the agreement makes interesting reading, as it sets out not just the physical boundaries in this new world, but the ways in which the English and Danes were to behave towards one another:

> This is the peace which King Alfred and King Guthrum and the councillors of all the English race and all the people who are in East Anglia have all agreed on and confirmed with oaths, for themselves and their subjects, both for the living and for the unborn, who care to have God's favour or ours.
>
> First concerning our boundaries: up the Thames, and then up the Lea, and along the Lea to its source, then in a straight line to Bedford, then up the Ouse to Watling Street.
>
> Next, if a man is slain, all of us estimate Englishman and Dane at the same amount, at eight half marks of pure gold; except the ceorl who occupies rented land and their freedmen – these also are estimated at the same amount, both at 200 shillings.
>
> And if anyone accuses a king's thegn of manslaughter, if he dares to clear himself, he is to do it with twelve king's thegns. If anyone accuses a man who is of lesser degree than a king's thegn, he is to clear himself with eleven equals and with one king's thegn. And so in every suit which involves more than four mancuses; and if he dare not clear himself, he is to pay for it with threefold compensation, according to its valuation.
>
> And that each man is to know his warrantor for men and for horses and for oxen.
>
> And we all agreed on the day when the oaths were sworn that no slaves or freemen might go over to the army without permission, any more than any of theirs to us. If, however, it happens that from necessity any one of

them wishes to have traffic with us – or we with them – for cattle and for goods, it is to be permitted on this condition, that hostages shall be given as a pledge of peace and as evidence whereby it is known that no fraud is intended.

What was clear from this agreement was that further clashes between English and Danish men would bring costly legal proceedings into the fray. These values were set higher than ever before and were not discriminatory against one side or another. The message was clear. If you wanted to trade across the border, you could do so with permission and with witnesses, but you had to give hostages. If you wanted to visit the other side of the boundary, again, you needed permission to do so. If you took the life of a leading man from the other side, you could expect no sympathy from your king if proven guilty.

How long this agreement stood, we cannot say. But it must have bought time for both sides. During this time, it would be Alfred, with access to vast resources both natural and human, who would make the most of what was given to him. The spiritual and intellectual rebuilding of the kingdom of the Anglo-Saxons would now take place. An army of scholars and clerics, who could oil the machinery of government and rescue the devastated churches of the kingdom, would flock to Alfred's court. Alfred had not entirely forgotten the prophecy of Jeremiah, the promise of the punishments that would be handed to his people for their ungodly ways through the visitation of the pagan terror.

887–892 The Value of Learning

And I would have it known that very often it has come to my mind what men of learning there were formerly throughout England, both in religious and secular orders and how there were happy times then throughout England.

From Alfred's prose preface to the translation of Gregory's *Pastoral Care*

The Viking Wars of Alfred the Great

While the scribe of the *Anglo-Saxon Chronicle* busied himself with the movements of the Danish armies on the Continent and the recording of the deaths of some significant people in England in these mercifully quiet years of Alfred's reign, the influx of foreign scholars into Alfred's court and from across the kingdom had begun to take effect.

From Mercia, Wærferth, the bishop of Worcester who had been at the side of both Ceolwulf II and the Ealdorman Æthelred, came to Alfred. His home town of Worcester would now join the defensive network of burhs and the bishop would personally see to the work being undertaken. Wærferth would receive some valuable property from Æthelred in London as a gift, and there now began an association of Alfred's family with the community of Worcester, which would last for generations. Worcester would be the place where Alfred's grandson, Athelstan, would receive his education, and scholars from this great city would feature heavily in the recording of English history from the tenth to the twelfth centuries.

For his piety and skills in organisation, Alfred attracted the capable Plegmund to his side. Plegmund eventually became archbishop of Canterbury in 890, after the death of Archbishop Æthelred, who had remained in post despite his role in the Viking wars. The chronicles record that, at around this time, many visits were made to Rome with the alms of the West Saxons by carefully chosen West Saxon noblemen. Alfred was clearly buying papal support and with a new pope, Pope Formosus (891–896), the policy of giving gifts to Rome, perhaps the origin of the English custom of Peter's Pence, looked like it was paying off. In 888 it had been Ealdorman Æthelhelm of Wiltshire who had gone to Rome. Later, Ealdorman Beocca and Queen Æthelswith, Alfred's sister and the wife of the exiled Burgred of Mercia, took West Saxon alms to Rome. Æthelswith never got further than Pavia, as she died on her journey. The following year, no one took alms to Rome, but our chronicler is keen to point out that Alfred kept up his correspondence with the Holy See by sending runners with letters throughout the year.

887–892 The Value of Learning

Meanwhile, Asser himself was being recruited into the Alfredian court. Originally from Wales, this monk of St David's was thrust into the heart of Anglo-Saxon affairs and was richly rewarded for his troubles. Among his numerous contributions to posterity is his biography of the king, which, if it is indeed authentic, provides some unique insights into the wars of Alfred.

The call went out around Christendom for more help. Fulco, the archbishop of Rheims was beseeched for the services of Grimbald of St Bertin, to which he eventually agreed. Grimbald, a modest but talented man, became Alfred's own mass-priest. Fulco, who would have liked to have seen his man at Canterbury, was at least able to reflect on the value of having such a close personal contact with the king of the Anglo-Saxons, the one man who had beaten the Danes at a time when there was such trouble on the Continent. As well as Grimbald, there was John the Old Saxon, whose personal influence on the king became great indeed. He had come from the ancestral Anglo-Saxon areas of Germany and he was given the abbacy at the new monastery at Athelney. Here at Athelney, amid a community made up of foreign refugees from the Viking attacks in Francia and an assortment of other characters, including a Danish boy, John would attract a few enemies. Legend has it that he was forced to defend himself from two hired Gallic slaves who made an attempt on his life at Athelney. His strength prevailed and when the king heard of what had happened the conspirators were not treated with anything like sympathy.

Alfred realised that the secret of successful government was in literacy. This was not just true in respect of the Latin scholarship, which underpinned the campaign to produce more men of the cloth, but was true also of the native tongue, English. Alfred bemoaned the fact that there was such widespread illiteracy in his kingdom. He had complained that it had not always been the case and like any good Anglo-Saxon, spoke of a previous Golden Age, when things had been so much better. Within his own court, he set up a school for his own household and those of his nobles. Within this school a young Edward beavered away at his books. One day, he would need all the education he had received to govern a remarkable kingdom himself.

The kingdom of the Anglo-Saxons was not just bigger than the old West Saxon kingdom: it had more things going on in it. The campaign for widespread literacy was essential in that it will have made record-keeping and communication so much easier for the administration of the kingdom. For example, the new burhs, in which property deals and international trading took place, could not be properly policed without a literate reeve. Taxation required both literacy and numeracy. Grand projects, such as the fortification building programme, needed a virtual civil service to run them.

Any kingdom in expansion requires more officials to run it, more soldiers to defend it, and so forth. All this, of course, had to be paid for. Asser tells us that the burgeoning coffers of Alfred's kingdom were split in two. The income came from a number of sources. There were the traditional annual food rents, due to the king and collected by his officials, which historically arrived at the royal tuns on the hoof, but which might equally be commuted these days for a financial payment. There were the tribute payments from client leaders throughout western Britain and the money raised from taxation of trading activities in this busy new kingdom.

The two-part split of royal income meant that the first half was spent on secular affairs. This was then divided into three equal parts. The first of these was spent on supporting his fighting men and his noble thegns. Payment, it seems, was made by the king annually at Eastertide. His thegns would join him at court on a tripartite shift basis, so that after a month in service with the king they could return to their estates to manage their own affairs until called upon again. The second part of the secular fund was spent on sponsoring the craftsmen of the kingdom. These people produced riches not seen since the days of the jewellers of the era of the great Bretwaldas. For the king they produced rings, bookmarkers and sword embellishments, all fine gifts for a warrior-king to lavish on his followers. The remaining third of the secular funds was to be distributed among the increasing number of foreign visitors who came to southern England. They had heard of Alfred's capacity for gift-giving and his tenacious hunger for news of the world beyond the shores of England. After all, the pagan menace was carving swathes across Christendom just a few miles away over the English Channel.

The second half of the treasury's income was earmarked for God. The king's thegns were told to divide this half into four parts, the first of which would support the poor and needy of any race who came to him. The second portion would go to support the communities at Shaftesbury and Athelney, which had been set up by the king, while the third part would support the school, which had begun to bring so much learning to those who would surely need it. The fourth portion was divided among the religious houses across the new kingdom. The funds must have been more than adequate, since Asser says that Alfred was able to provide financial support for houses in Wales, Gaul, Brittany, Northumbria and even in Ireland.

So, as Alfred's kingdom busied itself with administrative affairs, the king devoted half of his time to the service of God. Soon the strength of his devotion would be tested again, but for now Alfred set about studying and learning Latin, so that he could, by his own efforts, translate for the people some of the greatest philosophical and religious texts of the early medieval era. And yet for all this remarkable work, which had been undertaken by his subjects over the previous decade, there was no way – except for the worst case scenario – of testing it. Just how would Alfred's new kingdom survive an onslaught like the one that nearly broke it in the 870s?

892–893 The Return of the Danes

Francia Survives

The chronicler's obsession with events in Francia pervades the entries for the years between 886 and 892. Asser too, sometimes adding a nugget or two of his own knowledge of Frankish affairs, followed the progress of the enemy overseas. In 886, the year in which Alfred had taken London, there had been a

The Viking Wars of Alfred the Great

Viking siege of Paris involving at least 700 ships. This force was half of the army that split in the autumn of 884, choosing to go to Eastern Francia as opposed to joining with the other half in the ill-fated attempt to take Rochester. Paris withstood the siege heroically, led by a man who would feature again in the history of the Western Empire, the redoubtable Count Odo. But the siege took its toll on the Parisians, lasting a whole year, and for that time access to the bridge across the river was denied to the citizens by the Vikings.

When they withdrew from Paris in November 886, the Vikings exacted a promise of tribute from Charles the Fat, and they left with his permission to ravage Burgundy that winter. They sailed up the Seine and then the Yonne further to the south. In January and February 887 the force fulfilled its desire to wreak havoc in Burgundy, before sailing back to Paris to receive its promised tribute. It then sailed to the mouth of the River Marne, finally arriving at what Asser calls the royal estate of Chézy. From here it continued ravaging in the region and was still at large, operating from a new camp on the banks of the River Loing, where it wintered in 888–889.

The chronicler tells us that six weeks before his death, Charles the Fat was deposed by his nephew Arnulf, the son of Carloman. Arnulf rose to the ascendancy at this time and dispossessed Charles of his kingdom. Arnulf agreed to a split of the empire five ways, among others he felt had a lesser claim to power in this tangled complexity of Frankish families. Arnulf argued that the others should hold their lands from him, since he was the only one of them born on the paternal side. In short, Arnulf succeeded to the Eastern Frankish Empire, while Rudolph of Burgundy took control of the Burgundy region, leaving Odo, the count of Paris (perhaps not surprisingly) to inherit the Western Frankish Empire and Guy, the duke of Spoletto and Berengar, the Count of the March of Friuli, fought each other regularly for control of Italy.

And yet, amid all this fuss over Frankish affairs, our chronicler is still able to add a significant piece of domestic news for the year 890. Guthrum, King Alfred's godson and near-nemesis, was dead. The exact date of the Dane's death is not known, but may have been in late 889. Other sources say that he was interred at Hadleigh royal vill, in his adopted East Anglia. Æthelweard is perhaps the most revealing commentator on the death of Guthrum. He says that the Dane had been the 'king of the Scandinavian English' and that 'his settlement lay principally in East Anglia for there he had had the first colony'. Hidden within this statement is something which, by the time of his writing in the late tenth century, was only too apparent to Æthelweard. Throughout the tenth century a great political battle would be played out across the north and Midlands of the expanded kingdom of the English. It would involve the sons and grandsons of Alfred, who would seek to drive a wedge between Scandinavian Dublin and York, thereby preventing a northern Scandinavian Empire threatening their power on mainland Britain. The campaigns of Edward, Æthelflæd and Athelstan, each of them the descendants of Alfred, would go a long way to defining the borders of what is now modern England. In a sense, they would complete the work Alfred had started. But Æthelweard knew very well that ranged against Alfred's heirs were ambitious Scandinavian leaders, whose pretensions to rule over the Scandinavian areas of England became their battle-cry. What the wise old chronicler is hinting at here, is that he knew Guthrum to have been one of the first of such pretenders. Æthelweard, descended from King Æthelred I, the brother of Alfred, for all his uncomfortable Latin phrases and tortured syntax, was one of the few writers of Anglo-Saxon England who could add political experience and personal knowledge to the chronicles he had before him.

Meanwhile, the fascination with the Continent remained, and with good reason. The force still at large in the region of Paris had been paid off by Odo in 889, when it had attempted to return. It then sailed away to the west. In fact, it sailed right to the very borders of Brittany, arriving at St Lô in 890. No one knows quite what the tactics of the Bretons were in expelling the raiders, but their love of cavalry, and the fact that their enemy was pursued into the River Vire, might indicate that the Vikings were unpleasantly surprised by the Breton attack. The defeat was so overwhelming for these hardened Scandinavian warriors that their leadership decided to return to the east and face an enemy it felt it could at least do business with, and whose tactics on the battlefield they were well acquainted with. And so to the Seine they returned yet again.

On around All Saints Day, 1 November 890, the Vikings moved out from their Seine encampment and went east up the Oise, establishing a camp at Noyon, where they spent the winter devastating the area before moving off in the summer of 891 to Liège. Sometime in June that year they came across a Frankish force and surprised and defeated it. Arnulf took note. The Vikings headed for Louvain on the River Dyle, where they set up camp for the winter. Arnulf was nothing like his uncle. Negotiation came a poor second to the concept of giving battle. Besides, he had much to prove to his contemporaries. With a combined force of Saxons, East Franks and Bavarians, he fell upon the enemy sometime between August and November of 891. Curiously, the accounts record that Arnulf gave battle to the Viking mounted arm before their ships had arrived by sea. This might indicate a number of things: first, that the Vikings' experience in Brittany may have taught them further of the value of the horse in mobile warfare; and second, that if an enemy of the Vikings could drive a wedge between the land-based and sea-based wings of their operation, he might achieve victory that much easier. Louvain, by all accounts, was a massacre, a true bloodbath. We know nothing of the tactics used at the battle but the nature of the victory gave heart to a Christian kingdom long beset by the pagan menace. The river, we are told, literally ran red.

A Combined Attack

While Christendom rejoiced at the news from the banks of the Dyle, one leader in the west had his eye fixed on a new problem, just as serious as the one posed by the Louvain Vikings. Odo of Paris was watching a man who had slipped in and out of Scandinavian legend in his own lifetime, a man whose colourful Mediterranean campaigns had given him a fearsome reputation. The hardened campaigner Hæsten has a

892–893 The Return of the Danes

background swathed in deliberately orchestrated mystery. He may have been the leader who sacked Luna in northern Italy, mistaking it for Rome back in the early 860s. He was also apparently active in the river valleys of the Loire and Sarthe in the mid-860s, offering his services to paying rival Frankish nobles as it suited him. His shadowy presence in Continental records demonstrates that, for the most part, this extra-ordinary figure was often in touch with the leaders of the main Viking forces in Francia. Hæsten was indeed well-connected in the Scandinavian world, but from 892 he and some of his associates would share a very similar future together, not in Francia, but in England. To give us an idea of the sort of figure Hæsten was, Sir John Spelman, Alfred's biographer, adds a neat account:

> [the Vikings] had, under the leadership of Hastings [Hæsten], by the space of twelve or thirteen years together, to and fro ravaged all those countries up the Meuse, the Scheld, etc. and again the Sene, the Marn, the Sonne, the Lone, etc. and consumed to Ashes in that waste of theirs above 900 Houses of Religion.

Hæsten was in Amiens when news of the colossal defeat on the banks of the Dyle was brought to him. As if this were not enough, the famous warrior's scouts told him that the hero of Paris was on his way with a force to attack him. Things were clearly changing in Francia. The days of the conciliatory nego-tiations of Charles the Fat were well and truly over. The new bloods in France were keen to establish supremacy at the edge of a sword, and their enemy, who always chose to avoid pitched battles where they could, represented an opportunity for the numerous Frankish leaders to display their credentials in a competitive world. And here was Odo bearing down upon the great Hæsten. As it happened, Hæsten was able through skilful use of his own covert forces to surprise Odo's guards and stave off a defeat that might have matched the catastrophe of Louvain. But one thing was clear. After years of easy pickings, Francia was no longer a viable objective in the Viking mind.

The Viking Wars of Alfred the Great

Perhaps it was the sighting of a comet at Easter 892 that alerted the scribes of Alfred's court to what was about to happen. Or perhaps it was straightforward intelligence gathered by the king of the Anglo-Saxons, whose court was now brimming with international guests. Whatever the reason, the scribe compiling the *Anglo-Saxon Chronicle* for the year 892 stopped dead in his tracks. The fury of the Northmen had returned to England.

Those who had suffered defeat at the hands of Arnulf were the first to move. They went west to Boulogne. Here they received help from a local population only too willing to aid them on their way to a foreign country and out of harm's way. Ships were built for them, enough to carry their horses and attendant paraphernalia. It is almost as if it was known that the place they were going to had been stripped of its resources by the Anglo-Saxon king. All 250 ships left Boulogne for the south coast of Alfred's kingdom. They arrived at the mouth of the River Rother, then known as the River Lympne. Here, where the great wooded area known as the Weald finally runs out of steam after stretching a vast 120 miles from east to west, sat a little Alfredian fort. It was not one of the great forts of Alfred's building programme, but must be categorised as a burh nevertheless. Asser's groans that people were not pulling their weight in terms of fortress-building must have seemed doubly pertinent to the wise old scholar when the enemy sailed up the Rother estuary. The small fortification known as Eorpeburnan in East Kent was incomplete when it was attacked in the autumn of 892. Not only was it incomplete, but on landing there, the Danes discovered to their amusement that it was manned only by a handful of peasants whom they gleefully put to the sword. If this was a typical example of the defences the Anglo-Saxons had prepared for themselves, then conquest and settlement should be easy here. So much for the stories told by traders who had crossed the Channel over the last few years and spoken of the great works of the English. Having slaughtered the workers at the half-made burh, the Danes thought better of converting what they must have thought was a pathetic fortress for their own use and preferred instead to set up a fortification of their own making at nearby Appledore, probably along the lines of the ones other forces had set up at Reading and Fulham in recent years.

As if this was not enough, Alfred, on hearing the news that one of his fledgling forts was being overrun, must have shuddered at the news that Hæsten had brought with him eighty more ships and sailed up the Thames Estuary, setting up camp at Middleton, or Milton Regis, just across the River Swale from the Isle of Sheppey. Alfred was caught in a strategic dilemma. If these two forces situated on the north and south Kentish coasts were to shake hands with one another, a whole corner of Alfred's kingdom would be cut off. Furthermore, these two forces were probably both mounted and capable of supporting their land-based actions with sea support. There was one other worry for the king. Guthrum may be dead, but there were enough Danes settled in the Midlands and north of England to present a credible threat to the English king if they chose to support the newly arrived armies. What happened next in the landscape of southern England was a very different war to that which had occurred in the era of Ashdown and Edington.

Strategy and the Landscape

Alfred's initial reaction to the new threat seems to have centred on negotiation. During the winter of 892–893 he extracted oaths from the Northumbrian and East Anglian Danes and managed from the latter to secure six preliminary hostages, a move designed to secure a Danish agreement not to attack. Moreover, the arrival of Hæsten seems to have worried Alfred enough for him to send messengers to Milton Regis with an offer that had eventually worked so well with Guthrum. Hæsten would take up Christianity (if he had not done so already) and his sons would be baptised. He would therefore be a Christian leader in a Christian land and would hopefully be bound by the same sorts of obligations that had kept Guthrum more or less at bay for so many years. Alfred would stand as godfather to one son and Æthelred, Lord of the Mercians, to the other. The ceremonies went ahead, presumably with the same gravitas as in the days immediately after Edington. But Hæsten would not have looked at it in the same way as Guthrum had done. For a start, there was no kingdom waiting for him. He would have seen the whole thing as an elaborate bribe to get him out of Alfred's hair for a while. Hæsten went along with it all for the time being. His sons became the godsons of the two main Anglo-Saxon rulers and as he withdrew his fleet northwards to Benfleet in Essex, he must have sent out messengers to the East Anglians and Northumbrians to solicit their support for his new plans. It had been to prevent this very occurrence that Alfred had secured the loyalty of these other groups. But would the northerners break their promises?

History did indeed repeat itself. Most likely it was the East Anglians who were first to renege. The scribe of the *Anglo-Saxon Chronicle* returned to his work after the upheaval of 892 and recorded that, whenever the newly arrived armies went out on raids, they were either accompanied by the other Danes of England or that these others went out separately at the same time.

Alfred had already realised he had to act militarily even before Hæsten's negotiated removal to Benfleet. He had wedged himself directly between the two main invading forces, taking up a position somewhere in the Wealden forest, which had enough good trackways for his army to head either north or south should the necessity arise. His main concern was to prevent these two forces linking. The site of the Alfredian encampment during this stand-off in the Kentish countryside is probably Bredgar on the North Downs. If this was indeed the place where Alfred kept his eye on developments, he would have been able to see Milton Regis with the naked eye from this high vantage point. Behind him, and to the south, along the old Roman trackway leading from Rochester in the north to Hastings in the south, the king had almost certainly spread out a series of mounted patrols screening the north–south axis. These would have been backed up by the garrison at Hastings and smaller forces, possibly stationed at Benenden and Newenden further to the north, whose job must have been to contain the Appledore Danes.

A game of cat-and-mouse had then ensued in the countryside. The Appledore force during the spring of 893 went out in mounted groups, raiding through the Wealden forest on whichever side was undefended, and they were, in turn daily, harassed and chased by Anglo-Saxon mounted groups in combined operations with burghal garrison forces. Sometimes these operations went on well into the night. According to the chronicler, this tactic, along with the new reforms in Alfred's army system and his strategic positioning were enough to prevent both invading armies from going out in force more than twice. These occasions had only been at their first arrival when the English army was yet to be assembled and later when the armies attempted to abandon their strongholds en masse. In between those times effective strategic manoeuvre had been made impossible.

But the Appledore force had clearly been able to communicate in some way with Hæsten. Their raiding activities in the southern shires had won them considerable booty, and we are told that they wished to take this cargo across the Thames into Essex to meet with their ships. It is possible that the Appledore Danes had sent their ships around the coast to meet with the forces of Hæsten and the East Anglian Danes, in what was fast becoming a huge and politically viable gathering of what, at first, were disparate groups of people.

893 Edward the Elder

A Mistake at Thorney Island

And so the mounted portion of the Appledore Danes, while trekking their way beneath the Wealden forest, decided to turn to the north and attempt to find a ford across the Thames. Æthelweard shines some light on what happened next and on who was responsible for it. Onto the stage of Alfred's Viking wars stepped his eldest son Edward. The young ætheling Edward in 893 was embarking on a career that would make him more powerful than his father. He gained his eponymous name later in the tenth century, when scribes named him 'the Elder', probably in order to distinguish him from Edward the Martyr (975–979), another famous tenth-century king. Edward the Elder's contribution to the formation of the nation of England was no smaller than Alfred's. Æthelweard, writing with hindsight in full knowledge of what Edward would later achieve in the Midlands and in the north of England, is curiously the only near-contemporary source to account for his part in the campaigns of 893. Ironically, and infuriatingly, Æthelweard's text, so often vilified for its tortured Latin, is at its most obscure at this point in his chronicle, and in the form in which it came down to modern times, it even has groups of words missing. But there is enough to suggest that the young ætheling, who had already begun to appear on his father's charters as a witness with the suffix *Filius Regis*, was every bit the warrior leader his father would have expected:

> These matters are then made known to Prince Edward, the son of King Alfred. He had just been conducting a campaign throughout the southern parts of England; but afterwards the western English are also equipped. The engagement takes place at Farnham with the dense throngs shrieking with threats. Without delay the youth jump to it; attacked with weapons, they [words missing], they are duly liberated by the prince's arrival, just as, after the usual onslaught of predators, animals are taken back to the pastures with the shepherd's help. There the tyrant [the Viking leader] is wounded; they drive the filthy crowds of his supporters across the River Thames into northern parts . . .

To this interesting intervention by the dashing ætheling the scribe of the *Anglo-Saxon Chronicle*, without naming Edward, adds one important fact. The English army was entirely mounted. We can permit ourselves to imagine a scene whereby a highly mobile fresh force, consisting of Edward and his retainers and their own men, tied by the obligations bound up in lordship rites, overtook on horseback a tired and bedraggled force, laden with too much booty to escape the English. When Edward's men had gained the tactical position their mobility had afforded them, they dismounted and moved into the thick of battle. On being defeated, the Danish force with its wounded leader abandoned its booty, all of which was recovered by Edward, and fled north to the Thames, crossing where there was no ford, so great was their panic. Soon, the harassed Danes found their way along the River Colne into Buckinghamshire, presently making camp on an island near Iver known as Thorney.

The battle of Farnham had demonstrated something. No enemy army could move across Alfred's new kingdom with

An Anglo-Saxon Cavalry?

By the 890s Alfred's military reforms had included the instigation of a new office of king's horse-thegn. This was an office similar to that of the Carolingian Marshal and probably involved a logistical role with respect to the supply of fodder for a campaigning army. By the time of the reign of Alfred's grandson Athelstan (924–939) the value of the horse becomes clear. In 926 Athelstan received by way of a gift from Hugh, Duke of the Franks (d. 956) 'many swift horses with their trappings, champing at their teeth'. It was a gift which had consequences. By 937 many of the descendants of these animals were ready for a grand campaign in the north of England which would be celebrated for centuries. Athelstan introduced laws restricting the sale of horses in his kingdom, one law stating 'that no man part with a horse over sea, unless he wish to give it' and another which said that every landowner should provide two well-mounted men for every plough in his possession. Clearly, the use of horses in a military context in Anglo-Saxon England was widespread. However, there is no evidence that the mounted Anglo-Saxon warrior was employed in a true cavalry role on the battlefield. The likelihood is that mounted infantry were widely employed by the English armies of the period but it was not until the era of the Norman Conquest and the introduction of *milites* that mounted warriors were deployed to charge against an enemy on the battlefield itself.

impunity. Small raids along the Wealden forest edge at its eastern limits were one thing (and even these would be challenged), but dare the enemy move in large groups westwards, then the organised forces of the family of the king would fall upon them. So, with the Danes licking their wounds on Thorney Island, could the English claim a real victory?

Edward settled down to besiege Thorney. He knew the Danes were going nowhere for a while, as their leader was still incapacitated. Alfred himself sent messengers to Edward informing him he would be relieved soon. But the clock was ticking. Alfred's new military system had one serious flaw in it. Edward's force was now near to the end of its tour of duty. It was also running out of supplies. Soon, his men would return home to take up their other obligations under the new system, leaving a gap in time if Alfred did not arrive soon. Disaster then followed. The English strategic advantage was undone by a series of events.

Acting in concert, the Northumbrian and East Anglian Danes, who had sworn the usual promises and handed over hostages to Alfred earlier in the campaign, chose this moment to break their agreement. The coast of England was now swarming with the vessels of the Danelaw, led by a man called Sigeferth. When it became clear to Alfred that the destination of these 140 ships was in the west of his kingdom, he was caught on the horns of a dilemma. One hundred enemy vessels sailed to Exeter on the south coast and another forty came to Pilton on the North Devon coast. It may even be that the arrival of the Northumbrian and East Anglian fleet in Exeter finally persuaded Asser, who was possibly writing from Exeter at this time, to put down his quill and abandon his *Life of King Alfred*. Once again, like Guthrum had done during the prelude to Edington, the enemies of Alfred were trying to open more than one front. The question was, how would the king react to it this time around?

Surprise in the West

Alfred hastened to Exeter, but before he did so, he sent a small detachment to London, to the garrison commanded by

893 Edward the Elder

Æthelred of Mercia. Despite being alerted to the problem there was little the Mercian ealdorman could do with the Thorney force, as Edward was already negotiating the departure of the Danes with the usual exchange of hostages and swearing of oaths. The Danes fled to Hæsten's side at Benfleet, where a great force was gathering, consisting of Hæsten's original contingent and the remainder of the Appledore force that had not gone on the fateful Farnham raid.

Æthelred chose to gather his garrison force, collecting some reinforcements from the west, and headed out to Benfleet. It was now down to the Mercian ealdorman to deal with matters in the East. When he got to Benfleet, Æthelred could not believe his luck. Hæsten was out on a raiding mission with some of his men and was some distance from the Danish base, penetrating deep into the Mercian parts of the new kingdom of the Anglo-Saxons. There were however, a large number of Danes left at Benfleet, and the *Anglo-Saxon Chronicle*'s account of what happened there gives a glimpse as to the make-up of the forces ranged against Alfred:

> Hæsten had made that fortification at Benfleet earlier, and was then off on a raid and the great raiding-army was in occupation. Then they [the English] went up and put that raiding army to flight, broke down the fortification and seized all that was inside it, both money and women and also children, and brought all into London town; and all the ships they either broke up or burned or brought to London town or to Rochester.

The Danes had brought everyone with them, including, in some cases, their families. It would appear that they were intent on settlement in England, having been finally defeated on the other side of the English Channel. But now they faced another defeat square in the face. The Mercian ealdorman had seized all he could and had skilfully divided those ships he decided not to break between himself and Alfred. But there was something else. Æthelred had captured Hæsten's wife and children, one of whom, we might recall, was Æthelred's own godson.

The Viking Wars of Alfred the Great

The captives were sent to King Alfred. They were sent in the hope their presence at the king's court as hostages would bring Hæsten quickly to heel. But Alfred did not view it that way. Instead, he returned Hæsten's family to him and included additional gifts in the gesture. Perhaps Alfred was simply honouring his earlier agreement like a good Christian ruler should do, or perhaps there was a deeper message being sent out to Hæsten. Either way, Alfred clearly had no need for the hostages. For Hæsten, this campaign was turning into one of many surprises.

When he returned to Benfleet and was reunited with his family, Hæsten must have realised the nature of the calamity that had befallen him and appreciated the mercy of the king. He gazed out over the smouldering wrecks of some of his ships and viewed the broken fortification and the sorry warriors who had earlier been put to flight and separated from their families. But he was not to be beaten. He regrouped what was left of the combined fleet and sailed it a short distance to Shoebury. From there he called again for the East Anglian and Northumbrian Danes, who answered in the affirmative. It was clear to the old warrior that Alfred's kingdom was too strong to conquer using the tactics of yesteryear. Even with the king away on operations in the west – a deliberate Danish plan to separate English forces and weaken any resistance to conquest – there were still the armies of Æthelred and Edward to deal with. Not only this, but there seemed always to be a fortress or a mobile garrison somewhere in the landscape.

Starvation at Buttington

So, with his new reinforcements, Hæsten tried something quite different. Mercia was certainly defended on the south-west side of Watling Street, but Hæsten must have thought that he stood a better chance of establishing himself in the western areas of the kingdom, in much the same way as Guthrum had positioned himself by threateningly hovering above Wessex in 878. So, while Alfred sat outside Exeter watching another Danish army flee to its ships, Hæsten made a bold decision to go with his people, newly reinforced by the East Anglian and

Northumbrian contingents, on a dangerous march to the west. Quite what Hæsten was hoping for in the west is a mystery. The Welsh princes were pretty much in league with the king of the Anglo-Saxons, now that the wars of the sons of Rhodri Mawr were over. It is even possible that, when they set out, these Danes were intent on aiding their compatriots in the Exeter area. Whatever his reason, Hæsten and his force left Shoebury and travelled up the Thames Valley, carefully avoiding any of the Anglo-Saxon fortifications along the way. But as the Danes found themselves turning up the River Severn, the dangers of this extraordinary mission became evident.

What happened next, according to Æthelweard, became 'vaunted by aged men'. England, a country in the making, was learning to destroy its enemies. The 'famous' Ealdorman Æthelhelm of Wiltshire, who had taken West Saxon alms to Rome for his king back in 887, 'made open preparation with a cavalry force' and joined forces with the loyal Ealdorman Æthelnoth, who probably commanded an infantry army. Together they gathered all the king's thegns. They also gathered the garrisons occupying burhs east of the River Parret, and from both west and east of Selwood, and from those north of the Thames and west of the Severn. As if this were not a big enough force, they were soon joined by Æthelred of Mercia himself, who had his own large army in tow. But there was one more piece of devastating news for the Danish scouts, who had been looking over their shoulders at the great force now gathering against them. Their enemy now seemed to include a Welsh contingent. Any hope of alliance with the Welsh in this campaign was to be abandoned. Alfred had out-politicked the Danish leadership. At the banks of the River Severn, at a place called Buttington – probably at a site identifiable as the Buttington west of Shrewsbury – Hæsten made camp and waited. There are hints that Buttington may have been chosen because a small force of Danes had settled there a few years earlier and therefore this place might have been considered not just as a place of safety but a rendezvous point for all Danish forces involved in the complex strategic operation of outwitting the Anglo-Saxons. But now the combined army from the kingdom of the Anglo-Saxons had overtaken its foe from behind, divided itself into two forces either side of the river, and literally sat and watched the Danes as they stared starvation and defeat in the face. Moreover, any attempted breakout to the west was blocked by the forces of Mervyn of Powys. All this had been achieved without the presence of Alfred, who was absent in the west, such was the political unity he had inspired among the English. The sheer size and speed of concentration involved in this phase of the war almost certainly points to the realisation among the English that their Scandinavian enemies should not be allowed to unite.

Weeks passed. The English besiegers were supplied from their burhs with food and other goods, while the people inside the camp were compelled to eat their own horses. What happened behind the hastily constructed ramparts at Buttington was both a human tragedy and an emphatic military victory. The entombed Danish leadership was, by now, desperate. This mounted force, which had almost certainly been up to something else before the English caught up with them and turned them towards Buttington, now faced a slow and agonising death while their enemy looked on. One by one the Danes succumbed to death. In fact, in 1838, some 300 skulls attached to partial skeletons were found at the site, a possible testimony to the bloody struggle that was about to ensue. Something had to give, for the Danes knew they could not survive.

A decision was made – out of necessity rather than strategy – to attempt a surprise breakout. It was a predictably bloody encounter: hundreds perished in the attempt to save themselves. The decision seems to have been to strike out back to the east. That side of the river was heavily defended by the part of the English force that had split from the main army. Somehow, the Danes managed to draw themselves up in front of the English and the fighting that followed cost Ordheah, a king's thegn, his life. The Danes, like any cornered force, fought tenaciously, and while they did so, it seems many of their number were able to effect something of an escape. But it cost them dearly. None of the survivors would ever forget Buttington.

893 Edward the Elder

Chester

The Danes who survived the slaughter at Buttington knew exactly where they should head. Straight back east and to their Essex bases. Here, the bedraggled invaders met more reinforcements from East Anglia, and began to cool their heels as the year of 893 drew to a close. But it was clear to their leadership that they could not stay in Essex. It was too close to the network of English fortifications and too close to London for comfort. And so another decision was made. This time, perhaps acting on the advice of the surviving Northumbrian contingent, Hæsten made out for a distant ancient town he had heard of. It had been deserted since the days of the Romans, but its walls were still sound. If he could only set up camp there he might survive the winter and live to fight another day. He would be closer to his Northumbrian allies as well, closer still to the king of Gwynedd, from whom the Danes might have expected a little support. Also, just across the Irish sea sat the Scandinavian citadel of Dublin. But this ancient city in the north-west of Mercia, known to some still as the 'city of legions', was many miles away. In fact, it was back in the direction from which they had all just come. The city was Chester, situated at the foot of the Wirral Peninsula. If the Danes were to get there, then they must not take the same route they had taken when caught by the English fyrd. And so they made safe their women and children and even their ships. They spirited away these valuables into the East Anglian landscape and headed out to Chester via a huge arc to the north, once again desperately trying to avoid contact with the forces of the king of the Anglo-Saxons. They travelled as much by night as by day, so great was their concern not to get caught again. And they made it there – just. Alfred's forces had shadowed their prey to the north but had not managed to prevent them getting to Chester. Instead, Alfred reverted to the policy he had adopted outside Guthrum's camp after the victory at Edington. He killed the cattle the Danes had picked up on their journey and disposed of the straggling men outside the stronghold, and then took all the local produce for his own army and its horses.

All this destruction took the king just two days from the time he arrived at Chester. His own experiences had demonstrated to him that the cruel winter was capable of doing the rest of his work.

894 A Danish Rethink

And by the spring of 894 they knew it. Almost starved, the Danes moved out once again. They chose not to travel through the dangerous territory of Mercia to the east, but instead went deep into the heart of Wales, through the kingdom of a former ally, Anarawd ap Rhodri of Gwynedd, whose allegiance to King Alfred was probably brought about by his own despair at the lack of success of his Danish alliances. Southwards they marauded through the heart of the Welsh kingdoms, until they realised they could go no further for risk of being stopped by the allies of Alfred. The Danish leadership knew that it had to get back to the east, back to where their ships and supplies had been left. The route they took in order to do this reveals the successes of Alfred and his kinsmen in the campaigns to this date. The Danes turned on their heels in mid-Wales and headed north for Northumbria, skirting the top of Mercia before heading south down safer routes, through Lincolnshire and East Anglia, towards the island of Mersea in Essex. This circuitous route, perhaps the most evasive ever taken since the sons of Ragnar had landed in England in 865, was described by the *Anglo-Saxon Chronicle* as being necessary 'so that the English army could not reach them'. Soon this force would be joined by those who had given up their adventure in the west. The force that had been at Exeter had decided to sail back home. On their way back, they attempted to pick up some plunder by sailing straight into Chichester harbour but were thrown back by the forces of the garrison, losing many ships and men in an ill-fated effort against one of Alfred's better organised burghal defences.

Æthelweard records another force at large in the southern seas that year. This force was led by Sigeferth, a Viking leader from York who would soon replace the famous Guthfrith of York on the throne in the northern citadel. Sigeferth's contingent was probably the same force that had gone to the North Devon coast, as opposed to Exeter, some months earlier. Sigeferth's ambitions are unclear but they are likely to have been based on northern matters more than opportunism in Alfred's kingdom. As it happened, Sigeferth left the shores of North Devon and chose to sail to Scandinavian-held Dublin, where he took issue with yet another kinsman of Ivarr the Boneless, a leader named Sigtryggr. It was an important moment. The Scandinavian leadership would see the control of the twin cities of York and Dublin as vital in the successful creation of a Scandinavian empire in northern Britain. This would be the theatre for warfare of the new generation, as the line of Alfred sought to expand its power northwards and limit the influence of the Scandinavian warlords. But in the year of 894 the dreams of tomorrow's northern leaders must have seemed unthinkable to those stragglers who had remained at Benfleet when the flimsy and unprepared defences there were flattened by the resurgent local English population.

A good demonstration of how perspectives were beginning to change in these later campaigns is revealed by Æthelweard's account of the activities of Alfred's loyal ealdorman Æthelnoth. Sigeferth's presence in southern waters, particularly in the Bristol Channel, had been instrumental in the Northumbrian-backed push to unite all Scandinavian forces in the west and north-west against Alfred. The ealdorman set out directly for York. Quite what numbers he took with him we do not know, but he cannot have gone alone. At York Æthelnoth is supposed to have 'contacted' the enemy. Notwithstanding Sigeferth's activities in the west, we are told that there had been plundering in areas of Mercia between the River Welland and the wooded area of Kesteven, west of Stamford in Lincolnshire. The area in question corresponds to what was traditionally Rutland. It is possible that this area was in English hands after the treaty of Wedmore and that the ealdorman's visit to York was designed to warn the Northumbrians about their activities in the Danelaw as much as elsewhere. It is a measure of the strength of concern at Alfred's court regarding the growing power of Scandinavian Northumbria that Æthelnoth was sent on the journey at all. The visit reveals something else. With the old warrior Hæsten nearing the end of his days, the Anglo-Saxons probably now regarded York, under the leadership of Guthfrith, as the command and control centre for all this hostile activity against the kingdom of the Anglo-Saxons.

While all this was going on, the force that had returned to Mersea in Essex began looking for somewhere to spend the winter. The identity of the person who sent the Danes' families and valuables to the safety of East Anglia before telling his troops to sail up the Thames and into the Lea, is unknown. Hæsten disappears from the historical record at this point. It is possible that he died, perhaps from some of the hardships thrust upon him by the Anglo-Saxons, but one would expect the records to mention such a publicity coup. Nevertheless, his successor in the group of Danes at Mersea was no less decisive than Hæsten had been. In the autumn of 894 he chose to sail a route following exactly the boundary of the English and Danish territories as laid down in the treaty drawn up between Alfred and Guthrum. Once this group was 20 miles above London, at Hertford, it built a winter camp. It was an audacious move for a force that had seen so much disaster in recent times. Here it sat, threatening London, knowing it was outnumbered in a hostile landscape. London would be the final theatre of war in the long campaigns of Alfred the Great.

895–896 The Final Campaign

Autumn 895, Hertford

It must have seemed fairly simple to the Londoners in the summer of 895. The leading king's thegns of the burh would direct a force to go to the Danes' camp at Hertford and deal a fatal blow. As things turned out, it was an expedition that ended in catastrophe. Instead of besieging the place, the London contingent decided on a frontal assault of the Danes, who had used the previous months to refresh themselves and build sound defences. When the battle at Hertford was over, as many as four king's thegns lay dead on the field. It would not have impressed Alfred, who had shown he had a very different and very successful way of dealing with the Danes.

As autumn approached, Alfred realised that an active Danish force, based at Hertford, could easily destroy the fertile crops about to be harvested for the population in the burh. Alfred could not afford to let this happen, so when it came to the harvest, he placed his own army in the fields above London to prevent any such devastation. He was mindful of his own tactics against the Danes outside Chester and how successful it had been for him. But the king could not simply put a giant army in the field forever: something else was required as a deterrent; so Alfred, drawing on years of experience and on his wide travels, took yet another leaf out of the Carolingian manual of warfare. One day, according to the sources, he rode up the River Lea to see where the river could be obstructed, so the Danes could not bring their ships out. When he found the appropriate place, just as Charles the Bald had done on the Marne back in 862 and as Alfred's son Edward would also do on numerous occasions, he built twin fortifications straddling the river. As the construction began, the survivors of Buttington and Chester must have dreaded the outcome. They could not possibly stand another pro-tracted siege. It did not take long for a decision to be reached. Alfred had mastered the art of fighting the Dane. The Danes of Hertford broke camp and abandoning their ships to their fate, they fled, keeping north of the line created by the treaty of Wedmore.

Winter 895, Bridgnorth

The Danes fled as quickly as they could. Behind them, an Anglo-Saxon mounted army was in pursuit. Back at the Hertford camp the Londoners, many of them still smarting from the humiliation of defeat, now found themselves picking over their new prizes. Many Danish ships were seized and brought back to London to swell the numbers of Alfred's growing navy. Others, which were of no use to the English for one reason or another, were broken up where they were moored. With the English hot on their heels, the Danes managed to get to Bridgnorth on the River Severn, where they dug themselves in and prepared for the worst.

We know nothing of the diplomacy between Alfred and the leader of the force holed-up at Bridgnorth. We do not even know if they suffered the same sorts of hardships they had suffered at Buttington and Chester, although we can guess. What we do know is that, by the summer of the following year, they had split up and deserted the place, never to reform again. Some went back to their families in East Anglia, others melted away to Northumbria. Once again, those who had no money or portable wealth decided to try their luck abroad after what had clearly been a disastrous English campaign. This latter group fetched up with new ships on Christmas Day at Choisy on the Oise. *The Annals of St Vaast* mentions a Viking leader, Huncdeus, who had come from England. Perhaps this had been the leader who had taken over from Hæsten and threatened London? Perhaps this had been the man who at Bridgnorth had finally accepted Alfred's demands to leave his kingdom? We can only speculate as to the main reasons for the dispersal of the Bridgnorth force. The most likely explanation is the death in August 895 of Guthfrith of York and the need for the Scandinavians to reassess their leadership. In this respect Æthelnoth's visit to York in 894 may carry more weight than we can possibly know. Either way, the great land campaigns of the reign of Alfred the Great were over. He would spend the final three years of his life presiding over the spiritual and corporal defences of his now much expanded kingdom.

The contrast between the wars of 871–878 and those of 892–896 could not be greater. The first wars were characterised by frequent pitched battles, fought in desperation at a rate of attrition which, in the end, suited neither side and led to exhaustion and stalemate. Using cunning and political guile, Guthrum managed, in 878, to achieve his goal of removing Alfred from the government of Wessex and threw him into the cold Somerset wastelands. Ironically, the king of the Anglo-Saxons was only able to build a platform for a new type of warfare after winning back his throne by achieving victory in a good, old-fashioned, shield-wall clash at Edington. Here everything had been at stake, such are the punctuation marks of history. The winning of one key battle had made possible a persistent and organised military response to a foreign threat. Between 892–896 warfare in England would be characterised not by set-piece battles but by a combination of strategically placed and garrisoned forts, numerous mounted patrols, infantry armies and, of course, no shortage of the iron resolution that had carried the day at Edington.

The wars were over, but the dangers were not. As ever, these dangers were carried on the crest of the waves of the seas surrounding England in the form of the seafaring Danes from the north. Our last examination of the Viking wars of Alfred the Great concerns an unusual encounter on the waters off the south coast of England.

Aftermath

———➤-◉-◄———

896 The Navy in Action

The *Anglo-Saxon Chronicle* does not dwell on the nature of Alfred's victory over his enemies. In fact, the scribe who made the entry for 896 is far from cheerful. Although the last few Viking ships had already sailed over the horizon to continue their plunder in foreign places or returned to the meddlesome north, the chronicler concerns himself with the great loss of life among the English, brought about in that year by a pestilence among cattle and men. Leading bishops, key king's thegns and the town reeve of Winchester died in this year. One of the casualties, we are told, bore a title that hints at the importance of horses in the English system of war. Ecgwulf, the 'horse-thegn' seems to have been responsible for the mounted provision within the English army. This, like the role of the Carolingian *Marescalcus*, would have involved the entire logistical needs for each campaign.

Despite lamenting the loss of so many good Englishmen during the pestilence of 896, the chronicler tells us something else. For some years Alfred had been gathering vessels captured from the Danes. Now, in the aftermath of the great seizures made by the Londoners at Hertford, the king had even more vessels to study. Many of these vessels may not have been true Viking warships, but could have been of the Continental type, as they had been seized from Francia by Hæsten and his men in Boulogne in 892.

As the year drew on, the incidents of raids along the south coast increased. We are told that the culprits were once again the Northumbrian and East Anglian Danes, but the chronicler

Aftermath

noted that they were still using the ships they had built years ago. This was probably the catalyst for Alfred's construction of his navy. But what sort of navy would it be? Alfred knew he needed certain things from his ships. He needed them to be larger than the Danish ships, able to carry more men, and, if possible, they should be faster. It was a tall order. The traditional Viking ships of the northern seas were excellent and well designed. They were ocean-going vessels with a keel-built construction, but sufficiently shallow-drafted to be capable of river travel, right into the heart of enemy territory. They averaged around thirty oars per vessel at this time, but Alfred appears to have demanded sixty oars for his new design. The way in which a naval encounter was conducted during this era was that each side would try to lash its vessels to those of the enemy and attempt a boarding action. The hand-to-hand fighting would take place on the decks of the vessels, and was usually horribly bloody. Thus it made sense to build a vessel longer, larger, higher and faster than your enemy's ships, so that you had the advantage of numbers and height. Usually, however, in designing such a vessel, one aspect would have to be sacrificed for another. It would be difficult, for example, to build a huge ship and have it laden with warriors and expect it to clip through the water faster than a Viking vessel. The assertion of the chronicler that this is exactly what Alfred came up with, is surprising to say the least. This is not to say that Alfred was short of advice. Not only did he have his own shipwrights to talk to, there were plenty of Frisians in his court, too. The Frisians were close relatives of the English and their dominance of the trading networks of the North Sea and English Channel had been almost total for centuries. The kinds of vessels the Frisians built in the ninth century are thought to have been more like a precursor to the medieval cog than a Viking longship. These were flatter-bottomed, with a less pronounced keel, and high-sided. But Alfred was an independent thinker. We are told that the new ships were designed 'neither of the Frisian design, nor the Danish, but as it seemed to himself that they might be most useful'. These much vaunted vessels were built in the year 896. It was not long before they were tested.

The Viking Wars of Alfred the Great

Six Danish ships from East Anglia came to the south coast and ravaged around the Isle of Wight before moving on to the Dorset coast. Nine new vessels were ordered into action by the king. They sailed round the coast and found their prey in an unknown estuary on the south coast. Here, possibly at Poole Harbour in Dorset, the Danes were blockaded by Alfred's ships. The English discovered that the enemy ships were split into two groups. Three ships were drawn up on the shore, probably on rollers, while their crews were raiding inland, and the other three were afloat. The three vessels that were afloat realised they had to break out and so they took on Alfred's new vessels. Two of the Danish ships were boarded and their crews put to the sword, but the third vessel, whose crew was suffering the same fate as its compatriots, began to sail closer to the shore. The larger English vessels involved in the action ran aground on account of their much deeper draft. A shocked crew of just five shattered Danes were left with their vessel and made an escape, but the English had foundered. Six English vessels had grounded on one side of the estuary while three had got themselves stuck on the shore, on the same side of the estuary where the remaining three Danish vessels were beached. Despite an impressive display of hand-to-hand fighting, the English had not exactly come out of this encounter with good grace. Their vessels were proving cumbersome. And it was not over yet.

The crews of the three Danish ships out raiding in the countryside could not believe what they were seeing. On their side of the estuary were three stranded English ships whose crews had no hope of receiving help from their comrades on the other side. The tide was going out and it was a golden opportunity. The Danes, who were on foot, approached the English vessels and mounted an attack. The attack was successful and from the list of casualties we can deduce that the Frisian element of Alfred's new navy was very important to him. There perished the king's reeve, Lucaman, Wulfheard the Frisian, Æbbe the Frisian and Æthelhere the Frisian, along with a member of the king's own household. The fighting was fierce and cost the Danes 120 of their number and the Anglo-

Aftermath

Frisians sixty-two of theirs. It was a costly victory for the Alfredian navy. The final ignominy was that, what remained of the Danish crews were able to get away before the English, as their vessels were lighter and floated sooner on the rising tide. Besides, if they had been initially beached on rollers, as is likely, they could have been pushed out to sea that much quicker as the tide came in. And so we can imagine that, struggling with their wounded and wrestling with their huge ships, the English looked mournfully on the waters lapping at the base of their hulls as the Danes set sail and broke away from what was supposed to have been a blockade. The numbers are perhaps significant. If there were enough Danes to man the three ships that left the embarrassed English still wading through the mud, and if the Danes did lose 120 men, then the size of each crew on the Danish side must have averaged around forty-five.

But it was hardly a matter for Danish celebrations: they had received a mauling from an enemy who seemed to have an organised fleet. The Danish survivors of the naval battle of 896 will have learned much about the weakness of their enemy's vessel design, but will also have been surprised at the seaborne challenge to their usual tactics of coastal raiding. The vessels that rowed away from the encounter seem to have been insufficiently crewed to prevent two of them running ashore in Sussex. These unhappy crews were captured in Sussex and taken to King Alfred in Winchester. Here they were shown little mercy and hanged. Just one ship returned to East Anglia with a pathetic excuse for a crew. The story these wounded men would tell their countrymen would not be an easy one to bear. It would be some time before such raiding tactics were tried again. For all its clumsiness, for all of its seeming incompetence, Alfred's navy had made its mark. We do not know if there were further refinements to the design of the ships in the fleet over the next few years, but we are told that no fewer than twenty ships perished along the south coast of England in 896. A more enigmatic statement there could not be, but it is interesting that, for the rest of his reign, the southern shores of Alfred's kingdom are not recorded as being attacked from the sea.

The Viking Wars of Alfred the Great

897–899 Peace and the Dark Horizon

The final years of Alfred's reign are somewhat skirted over by the writers of the day. The king turned his energies to a combination of things, including the granting of more prize waterfront allotments in London to his senior archbishops, bishops and ealdormen, as well as concentrating on his own writings. Alfred, mindful that his own life would soon draw to a close, seems to have tried to make certain the smooth ascendancy of his proven and tested son, Edward. Alfred held high hopes for the future of the kingdom of the Anglo-Saxons, and as it turned out, his faith was not misplaced. Edward had already – albeit illegitimately – provided Alfred with a grandson. Born around 895 to Edward and Ecgwynn, a beautiful but enigmatic figure not of the royal stock, the young boy Athelstan quickly became a favourite of the old king. He bore the name of Alfred's own brother – and the very name given to Guthrum on his baptism. Historians told that Alfred even bestowed many of the riches given to him by the pope upon this boy and that Athelstan even underwent something of an inauguration ceremony. The problem the line of Alfred faced, however, after the great king's death, was not so much from the Danes, but came instead from within the extended family of Alfred himself. This is how Anglo-Saxon politics worked. We might recall the shadowy figure of Æthelwold, the son of Alfred's brother Æthelred I, who had long been aggrieved at the terms of Alfred's will. The overt pronouncements towards the end of Alfred's reign of the passing of power down through Alfred's son and possibly first grandson will have annoyed Æthelwold intensely. Edward, from around 898, just a year before his father died, seems to have been made a co-ruler in preparation for his accession to the throne.

Æthelwold sat and fumed until he could hatch a plot to challenge Edward. Alfred the Great, the 'unshakeable pillar of the western peoples' died on 26 October 899 and his body was taken with great ceremony to the Old Minster at Winchester, only to be translated by Edward a few years later to the New Minster there. Æthelwold made his move. He gathered supporters and took over the royal estates at Wimborne and

Aftermath

Christchurch (then known as Twinham). Perhaps it was a move taken from the Danes' manual of warfare. By taking Wimborne, the ancient symbolic burial place of West Saxon kings, Æthelwold was staking his claim to legitimate power. Here, in this ancient seat, the pretender to Edward's throne announced that he would 'live or die' there. But if Æthelwold thought he could stir dissension in the witan or among the West Saxon nobility he was sorely mistaken. Alfred had changed the human geography of the south. There were too few supporters for the son of Æthelred I to rely on, and so it seems he turned to a course of action which, had it succeeded, might have changed that map forever. As the army of Edward set up its camp at Badbury Rings, overlooking the somewhat smaller force of the pretender, Æthelwold made a dash for it. He was more or less on his own when he took his horse and stole away from the royal army. He even left behind him a nun he had abducted from a nunnery without the king's leave and against the advice of the bishop. The taking of this woman – about whom we know very little – was seen as an act of contempt against the king and will have angered him greatly. Edward could however, perhaps be forgiven if he felt that this challenge to his power was little more than a sideshow, but history would prove it to be far more than this.

If the new king of the Anglo-Saxons could have been sure where Æthelwold was going he might have tried harder to stop him. After a few days and nights Æthelwold fetched up in Northumbria, where he made a serious impression on the Danes. Despite the political power the Danes held in Northumbria, there was still a local Anglian population whose opinions the Danish leadership always needed to be wary of. The Danes quickly submitted to Æthelwold and accepted him as their king. It was an extraordinary achievement and will have sent the alarm bells ringing around the halls of Winchester. But Æthelweard records an interesting phenomenon. There was 'a very great disturbance', he says, 'amongst the English, that is the bands who were then settled in the territories of the Northumbrians'. What promises had Æthelwold made to the pagans of the north? Whatever the agreement, it seems to have upset the local population enough for them to brave a protest or two against their overlords. Perhaps the successor of Sigeferth in York, a figure by the name of Cnut, had a part to play in all this upheaval at the arrival of Æthelwold. The chronicler Æthelweard says no more on the matter and only gives us glimpses of what Æthelwold got up to in the few years after Alfred's death. This is probably because this noble scribe was himself descended from the line of Æthelred I and was writing at a time when the line of Alfred had more than simply won its argument. But it remains the case that, for the opening years of the tenth century, Edward, son of Alfred, had an Englishman and not a Dane as his most dangerous enemy.

Æthelwold went missing from the historical record for a year after he ran off to the Northumbrians. It may be that he was gathering reinforcements for his plans abroad, perhaps even in Denmark. He turned up again in Essex with a force of such size as to persuade the East Anglian Danes to side with him. There are tantalising references to Æthelwold as 'king of the Danes' and 'king of the pagans' in the sources. Had he really abandoned Christianity in his bid to wrest the throne from Edward with Danish help? Matters came to a head after an extraordinary raiding campaign masterminded by Æthelwold, which saw his army carve its way through parts of Edward's kingdom, culminating in a huge battle at the unidentified site of Holm. Here, many English fell on the battlefield, but perhaps most significantly, Eric, the Danish king of East Anglia and Æthelwold himself perished in the campaign.

The years that followed Holm were a little quieter for Edward. Both he and his sister Æthelflæd, and her husband Æthelred of Mercia, were able to consolidate the English holding south of the Danelaw, and through a process of persuasive argument in some places, were even able to buy back parts of the Danelaw from the Danes.

Once again, the political geography of England was changing. The kingdom of the Anglo-Saxons was now beginning to take shape as the kingdom of the English. Nor had it stopped expanding. Some of the Danish communities of the

Aftermath

north started to look to the southern English leaders for protection as a new threat, the Norseman, swept into York and began to add yet another dimension to the complexities of the northern world. Edward the Elder, his sister Æthelflæd, his son Athelstan, and Athelstan's half-brothers Edmund and Edred would lead the English charge to the north. Soon, it would all come to a spectacular head at a place lost to history, but whose importance was unequalled until the battle of Hastings. This place was Brunanburh. Today no one can positively identify the field upon which Athelstan won a decisive victory in 937 against a confederation of Vikings, Scots and Strathclyders. Serious candidates for the site of the battle of Brunanburh range from Bromborough on the Wirral to far-flung places in Scotland.

But with so much lost to us through the mists of time, there is still one thing that is obvious. Were it not for the English successes during the Viking wars of Alfred the Great, the victory at Brunanburh would not have been possible. There would not have been a kingdom of the Anglo-Saxons, no kingdom of the English and no England. Instead, the country would have been pulled inevitably into the Scandinavian world and from one coast to another, the names of places, people, and the type of language they spoke would have been changed forever. Even if one Scandinavian ruler had managed to exert his power over other competing polities, it is unlikely that the kingdom he would have presided over would have become England. That country owes its origins to the vision of King Alfred and his issue.

Generation after generation of historians, from Alfred's time to our own, have singled the great king out for his achievement. Royalist and Parliamentarian, Tory and Whig, Conservative and Liberal alike, all saw in Alfred the founding characteristics of the English people. As for his military skills, Alfred's education stood him perhaps in the best stead. He was able to organise on a grand scale great public works, was able to disseminate information and instruction throughout his kingdom; but most of all, he appears to have possessed the sort of personality which, even in his darkest days, people could not divorce themselves from. On 26 October 899 at the passing of Alfred, a fledgling nation took stock. A vision had once been seen by a king through the flames of destruction in a desolate place, when he was on the run from his enemies in his own kingdom. During a period that seemed like an age, the makeshift forges of Athelney island brought new weapons into the hands of the Anglo-Saxons. Armed with these, and with the prayers said for them at the church built in the same place, the warriors of Anglo-Saxon England had set out on a journey that brought them to Edington and a final showdown with Guthrum the Dane. None of them could have imagined the real importance of what they were doing. Between them the loyal forces of an extraordinary king had set out to create the kingdom of England.

Appendix I:
Orders of Battle

The lists below can only be educated guesses, so poor is the historical evidence for the presence of anyone beneath the rank of commander. For each battle, the probable commanders and subcommanders are listed. Known leaders are in normal text and proposed subcommanders are presented in italics. Each leader of the era will have brought to the battlefield all those who owed him service as part of their lordship bond. Depending on who the leader was, numbers in the retinue could vary considerably. The retinues would be made up of thegns and ceorls. Thegns would have been armoured and the lesser ranks unarmoured. Swords, spears and shields characterised the main weapon array of both sides, with the Danes also using an early form of their famous Daneaxe. Any evidence for mounted troops is also included below. In cases where a king was accompanied by his fyrd, or expeditionary force, this is mentioned. For the Great Heathen Army, and later, for the followers of the Dane Hæsten, it is assumed that the paucity of evidence for subcommanders and their followers should not be taken to indicate low numbers in terms of combatants. The size of the fortification at Shoebury should be evidence enough to suggest these armies were larger than recent arguments have suggested.

The Viking Wars of Alfred the Great

The Battle for York, 1 November 866

  ANGLIAN
  King Ælle
  Townsfolk of York
  THE GREAT HEATHEN ARMY
  Ivarr
  Halfdan
  Ubba

The Battle for York, 23 March 867

  ANGLIAN
  King Ælle
  (King) Osberht
  THE GREAT HEATHEN ARMY
  Ivarr
  Halfdan
  Ubba

Nottingham 868

  ANGLO-SAXON
  King Burgred of Mercia and his fyrd
  King Æthelred I of Wessex and his fyrd
  Ætheling Alfred of Wessex
  THE GREAT HEATHEN ARMY
  Ivarr
  Halfdan
  Ubba

The Battle of Englefield, 31 December 870

  ANGLO-SAXON
  Ealdorman Æthelwulf of Berkshire
  DANISH
  Detachment of Great Heathen Army possibly led by a *Jarl Sidroc* and one other jarl

Orders of Battle

The Siege at Reading, 3 January 871

ANGLO-SAXON
King Æthelred I of Wessex and his fyrd
Ætheling Alfred of Wessex
Ealdorman Æthelwulf of Berkshire
THE GREAT HEATHEN ARMY
Ivarr
Halfdan
Ubba
Bagsecg

The Battle of Ashdown, 8 January 871

ANGLO-SAXON
King Æthelred I of Wessex and his fyrd
Ætheling Alfred of Wessex
THE GREAT HEATHEN ARMY
Ivarr
Halfdan
Ubba
Bagsecg

The Battle of Basing

ANGLO-SAXON
King Æthelred I of Wessex and his fyrd
Ætheling Alfred of Wessex
THE GREAT HEATHEN ARMY
Ivarr
Halfdan
Ubba

The Viking Wars of Alfred the Great

The Battle of Meretun, 22 March 871

ANGLO-SAXON
King Æthelred I of Wessex and his fyrd
Ætheling Alfred of Wessex
Heahmund, bishop of Sherborne
THE GREAT HEATHEN ARMY
Ivarr
Halfdan
Ubba

The Unknown Battle of 871

Fought between the battles of Meretun and Wilton at an unknown site in Wessex whilst Alfred was burying his brother at Wimborne.
ANGLO-SAXON
Unknown Anglo-Saxon ealdorman
THE GREAT HEATHEN ARMY AND NEW DANISH ARMY
Ivarr
Halfdan
Ubba
Guthrum

The Battle of Wilton, May 871

ANGLO-SAXON
King Alfred of Wessex and his fyrd
THE GREAT HEATHEN ARMY AND NEW DANISH ARMY
Ivarr
Halfdan
Ubba
Guthrum
Anwend
Oscetyl

Orders of Battle

The Battle of Cynuit, *878*

ANGLO-SAXON
Ealdorman Odda of Devon
Unknown number of king's thegns
DANISH
Ubba

The Battle of Edington, May 878

ANGLO-SAXON
King Alfred of Wessex and his fyrd
Ealdorman Æthelnoth of Somerset
DANISH
Guthrum

Rochester, 884–885

ANGLO-SAXON
King Alfred of Wessex and his fyrd
DANISH
Hæsten

The Battle of Farnham, 893

ANGLO-SAXON
Ætheling Edward the Elder leading an entirely mounted
force
DANISH
Unknown Danish leader

The Viking Wars of Alfred the Great

Buttington 893

ANGLO-SAXON
Ealdorman Æthelred of Mercia and his fyrd
Ealdorman Æthelhelm of Wiltshire commanding an entirely mounted detachment
Ealdorman Æthelnoth of Somerset
Garrisons from east of River Parret, from west and east of Selwood and those garrisons from north of the River Thames and west of the River Severn
Ordeah, a king's thegn
Mervyn of Powys and his forces
DANISH
Hæsten
Other Danes already in residence at Buttington

Hertford, Autumn 895

ANGLO-SAXON
London Garrison
DANISH
Unknown Danish leader, possibly Huncdeus

Naval Encounter, South Coast of England 896

ANGLO-FRISIAN
Nine vessels (unknown Frisian commander)
Casualties on English side listed as:
Lucaman, King's Reeve
Wulfheard the Frisian
Æbbe the Frisian
Æthelhere the Frisian
Various members of King Alfred's household
Total 62 casualties
EAST ANGLIAN DANISH
Six Vessels
Unknown East Anglian Danish commander
Total 120 casualties

Appendix II:
Biographical Notes

Æthelnoth, ealdorman of Somerset (d. c. 894). One of Alfred's most reliable and loyal servants, this leading figure in West Saxon politics served his king during the dark days at Athelney in 878, and was instrumental in securing various military victories for Alfred during the era of the second invasions of the Danes. He led a force to Buttington in 893 and besieged the Danes there. The following year he took a force to York thus beginning – on behalf of a southern English king – a long history of dialogue, diplomacy and warfare between York and Winchester.

Æthelred 'Lord of the Mercians' (d. 911). Æthelred ruled Mercia after the death of Ceolwulf II in or around 879–880. He was not, however, a king, but ruled as an ealdorman. Æthelred recognised Alfred as his overlord and married Æthelflæd (d. 918), Alfred's daughter. The Mercian ealdorman played a vital part in bringing the Welsh kingdoms to heel and securing their allegiance to Alfred. He also was instrumental in chasing away the Danish threat to London and Mercia in the 890s. His wife continued to rule Mercia after Æthelred died and made fame for herself during the conquests of the Danish-held north in the early tenth century.

Æthelweard (d. 998). The great-great-grandson of Æthelred I of Wessex, Æthelweard was ealdorman of the western provinces in the late tenth century. He was well known for his

The Viking Wars of Alfred the Great

high political standing and his influence during negotiations during the second phase of Scandinavian incursions. Mostly, we are grateful to Æthelweard for a Latin translation of a lost version of the *Anglo-Saxon Chronicle*, which contains valuable additional information which would otherwise be lost to us. The work was dedicated to his cousin Matilda, the Abbess of Essen, who was a great-great-granddaughter of King Alfred. Predictably, his version of events reflects the sensibilities of the recipient of the gift.

Æthelwulf, king of Wessex (839–858). The son of the powerful West Saxon King Ecgberht (802–839), Æthelwulf was also the father of Alfred the Great. He was succeeded by four of his sons, of whom Alfred was the last. In 851 he won a renowned victory against the Vikings in England. In 855 he went to Rome and on his way back picked up a young bride in the form of Judith, daughter of Charles the Bald. However, a dispute among the West Saxon nobility and the rise to power of his son Æthelbald found him in political difficulties at the end of his reign.

Æthelwulf, ealdorman of Berkshire (d. 871). Æthelwulf made a name for himself during the early wars of Alfred the Great. Although he was ealdorman of Berkshire, a recently acquired West Saxon territory, Æthelwulf was in fact a Mercian. His military activities against the Great Heathen Army saw him excel in the art of the ambush, often catching his enemy unawares when they were out on reconnaissance or foraging missions. When he was killed at the battle of Reading, Æthelwulf was not buried locally but taken all the way to Derby, his ancestral home in the north Midlands, which at the time was known as Northworthy.

Asser (d. 908/9). Asser came from the monastery of St David's in the Welsh kingdom of Dyfed. King Alfred is said to have specifically sought out the services of Asser, having been impressed by him at a meeting in Sussex around the year 885. Asser wrote a *Life of King Alfred* in around 893, though some

Biographical Notes

historians doubt its authenticity. The work provides a wealth of additional personal information about the king, without which we would be very much in the dark as to his extraordinary character. Throughout his work, Asser reveals to his audience the Welsh place names of English towns, indicating that his readership was at least partially Welsh.

Burgred, king of Mercia (852–874). Burgred called upon Alfred's father, Æthelwulf, to help in his campaigns against the Welsh, which proved to be successful. Following these, Burgred married Alfred's sister in a bid to unite Wessex and Mercia. In 868, however, when the Great Heathen Army came to Nottingham, Burgred was forced to call again on the king of Wessex and his brother Alfred, who came to the town with a sizeable force, but soon returned home without offering battle. Later, in 874, Burgred was flung out of his kingdom by the Danes and took his bride with him. He was replaced by a puppet king, Ceolwulf II. Burgred never returned to England.

Ceolwulf II, king of Mercia (874–c. 880). Apparently descended from Pybba of Mercia, Ceolwulf II represented a rival family to the long-standing King Burgred (852–874). When Burgred was thrown out of his kingdom by the Danes in 874, Ceolwulf was offered up to the Mercians as a puppet king. Although the *Anglo-Saxon Chronicle* calls him a foolish king's thegn, Ceolwulf seems to have been able to defeat the Welsh, accounting for the death of Rhodri the Great. Later, at a battle in Conway, Ceolwulf was himself defeated by the avenging Welsh. After his death he was succeeded by Æthelred, Lord of the Mercians.

Ecgberht, king of Wessex (802–839). The grandfather of Alfred, Ecgberht, whose name means 'bright edge', was responsible for raising the power of Wessex above all other Anglo-Saxon kingdoms in England. Generations of historians accord to him the accolade of being the first king of all England, but this title should really be shared between his grandson Alfred and great-grandson Edward.

The Viking Wars of Alfred the Great

Edmund, king of East Anglia (d. 869). Edmund was killed at the hands of the Great Heathen Army in 869. Soon he gained a reputation as a saint among none other than the Danes themselves, who, by way of atonement, struck coins in his honour across the north and east of England. The monastery at Bury St Edmunds became one of England's great medieval communities. Edmund has often been held up as an ideal Christian king, as a result of his grisly death at the hands of pagans.

Edward the Elder, king of the Anglo-Saxons (899–924). Edward was the son of Alfred, who extended the domains of his father and secured the submission of a number of northern rulers in 921. As a young man he featured heavily in the second stage of Alfred's Viking wars. He defeated and pursued an enemy force at Farnham until it was chased north of the Thames. In later years, he would go on to be one of the most successful kings of English history.

Grimbald of St Bertin (d. 901). Grimbald was one of an army of Continental scholars who answered Alfred's call for help in the spiritual revival of his kingdom. He arrived in England around 887 and a letter survives from Fulco, archbishop of Rheims (883–900), who had been abbot at St Bertin, which acts as something of a reference for Grimbald. On the death of archbishop Æthelred of Canterbury in 888, Grimbald seems to have turned down the offer of the job.

Guthrum (d. 890). Guthrum, whose career in England is outlined in this volume, was Alfred's main foe for many years in the 870s and 880s. He had come with an earlier Danish army and had taken his own men to Cambridge in 874, where he set his sights on dismembering Wessex. He nearly succeeded but was thwarted at Edington in 878 by the man he thought he had previously eliminated, Alfred the Great. After this, Guthrum was Christened and baptised as Athelstan and settled to rule East Anglia as a Christian king. However, there is some evidence that Guthrum was still actively plotting against the English right up to his death. The treaty between Alfred and

Biographical Notes

Guthrum, which split the English Midlands into two halves, still survives.

Hæsten (d. *c*. 895). Another Scandinavian legendary hero who nearly became the second nemesis for King Alfred after Guthrum the Dane. A long-lived hero, he first appears in French records leading a combined Viking/Breton fleet up the Sarthe into Anjou in 866. But he had been active in the Loire Valley before then. He was always keen to get involved in politics, often joining sides with warring native factions. After Continental successes and failures he came to England in the early 890s and began a campaign against Alfred's reconstituted kingdom, but was chased around the country by Alfred and Æthelred's mobile armies. He had a naval base at Shoebury in Essex, part of which still survives.

Halfdan (d. *c*. 876). A semi-legendary son of Ragnar Lothbrok, Halfdan was instrumental in the early years of the wars of Alfred the Great. He led the Great Heathen Army from 865 against the old Anglo-Saxon kingdoms, and was responsible for the dividing of Anglian Northumbria among his own followers. Halfdan, along with his brothers, was known for his cruelty but was a clever military campaigner all the same. For the most part, Halfdan's attentions were very much centred on the northern world during this period, particularly around the Dublin–York axis, where so much blood would be spilled in the tenth century.

Ivarr the Boneless (d. *c*. 873). Another son of Ragnar Lothbrok, Ivarr was at the head of the Great Heathen Army that descended on England in 865. As with all Ragnar's sons, divorcing the myths from the truth is almost impossible. However, there are tantalising hints that this man who terrorised the British Isles was in fact brought to Repton in Derbyshire after his death in Ireland and buried under a pagan mound over an older Christian mortuary chapel. The meaning of his sobriquet 'the boneless' has been debated to this day, but may indicate either childlessness or extreme cruelty.

The Viking Wars of Alfred the Great

Ragnar Lothbrok, (d. *c*. 865). A classic figure from Viking legend, whose dates are uncertain. Apparently, he was king of Sweden, conquered Denmark, and travelled widely, causing stories to be told wherever he went. Some sources place his reign between 750–794 and others from 860–865. It is most likely he was active between about 835 and 865, when his encounter with the Northumbrian king Ælle famously saw him meet a sticky end in a pit of snakes. English legends say the arrival of the sons of Ragnar in East Anglia, in 865, with the Great Heathen Army, was the beginning of a mission of vengeance against the English for killing their father. In 845 Ragnar seems to have held Paris to a ransom of around 7,000 pounds of silver.

Ubba (d. 878). Another of Ragnar Lothbrok's sons and no less cruel than his brothers, Ubba's particular claim to fame as a commander in the Great Heathen Army was his role in the murder of St Edmund. This one event propelled an Anglo-Saxon king into sainthood and condemned Ubba to the darker side of history. Soon the Viking leaders of the north would strike coins in celebration of the slain Englishman, so great was their remorse. As for Ubba, his fate was decided at the battle of *Cynuit* in 878 on the north coast of Somerset, in the area around the mouth of the Parret. Here Ubba was slain by the men of Odda of Devon and the famous raven banner of the sons of Ragnar was captured by the English.

Appendix III:
Campaign Glossary

Ætheling – A term found in contemporary poetry indicating a 'good and noble man', but often, in reality, relating to princes of the royal line.

Burh – A fortified stronghold. These forts were built to the order of King Alfred across the ancient kingdom of Wessex and parts of English Mercia from around 880. They acted as places of secure refuge for the local population, but were garrisoned according to a carefully worked out formula. No burh was further than a day's march from another, and each garrison worked in close cooperation with the king's mobile field army and other garrisons, so that it was difficult for an enemy to travel across southern England without being intercepted. The total estimated garrison strength of the West Saxon burhs alone stands at an impressive 27,000 men.

Charter – Normally written on one sheet of parchment, a charter was a record of a land grant or privilege granted by the king to a person or religious community.

Danelaw – An area of the Midlands and north of England, which existed outside English West Saxon and Mercian legal jurisdiction in the ninth, tenth and eleventh centuries and beyond. The areas of the Danelaw are roughly equivalent to East Anglia, Yorkshire and Northumbria, plus the counties of central and eastern England.

The Viking Wars of Alfred the Great

Ealdorman – By Alfred's time these were leaders of individual shires within the kingdom.

Frisian – Close cousins to the ancestral English, the Frisians during this period were masters of the northern seas. Their homeland stretched from the Sincfal in the south to the Weser in the north. Frisian traders were responsible for the influx of a great deal of silver coinage back into the western economy.

Fyrd – The Old English term for a military expeditionary force. Much argument over its make-up has taken place in recent years, but essentially the fyrd consisted of an army bound by lordship ties.

Jarl – A Scandinavian word for a leader or 'earl', not to be confused with the modern English sense of the word 'Earl'. A jarl's social standing as a freeman was characterised by his warrior-like abilities.

King's Thegn (see also the definition of Thegn below) – Distinct from an ordinary thegn, the king's thegn makes his first appearances in West Saxon sources in the 830s, listed as witnesses to charters. They occupied a position of personal service to the king in the form of ministers. They swore an oath to love all he loved and hate all he hated. In return for their services they were rewarded by the king's protection. Among their duties were keeping the peace, trade transaction regulation when performing the reeve's duties and the collection of royal dues. Many king's thegns would have their own military following.

Lundenwic – The trading settlement at London that grew outside the Roman walls and to the west of the ancient city. Mentioned by the Venerable Bede, Lundenwic was abandoned when Alfred rebuilt the town as one of his burhs in 886. The settlement is thought to have had a population of around 5,000 at the time the Danes took refuge behind the walls of the nearby Lundenburh.

Thegn – Literally means 'one who serves'. A thegn would be a

Campaign Glossary

minor noble in his own right. As well as serving his lord or ealdorman, depending on his own personal bonds of lordship, a thegn would have his own retinue of people who owed him service. Military obligations were often placed on the thegns of Anglo-Saxon England.

Witan – A term that meant 'wise men'. The witan was a council that advised an Anglo-Saxon king and usually consisted of members of the royal household, senior leading churchmen and regional ealdormen.

Appendix IV:
Regional Lists

The lists below show the rulers of the various kingdoms in the period covered by this book. Alfred succeeded in melding the rump of English Mercia with the kingdom of Wessex, thus forming a whole new polity of which he was the first king. This kingdom was the kingdom of the Anglo-Saxons and it was the foundation for the kingdom of England. The son and grandsons of Alfred would enhance the territorial aspects of this kingdom and give it a new name, the kingdom of the English. By the end of the tenth century the English king would rule from the borders of Scotland to Cornwall.

Mercia

Beorhtwulf, king of Mercia (840–852)
Burgred, king of Mercia (852–874)
Ceolwulf II, king of Mercia (874–879/80)
Ealdorman Æthelred, Lord of the Mercians (*c.* 880–911)
Æthelflæd, 'Lady of the Mercians', daughter of King Alfred, wife of Æthelred (911–918)

Wessex

Ecgberht, king of Wessex (802–839)
Æthelwulf, king of Wessex (839–855 [to Rome], 856–858)
Æthelbald, king of Wessex (855–858 [subking], 858–860) (858, marries stepmother Judith)
Æthelberht, king of Wessex (855–860 [subking], 860–865)
Æthelred, king of Wessex (865–871)

Regional Lists

Alfred, king of Wessex (871 [begins his reign as king of Wessex, but then forms an expanded kingdom of the Anglo-Saxons]–899)

The Kingdom of the Anglo-Saxons

Alfred, king of the Anglo-Saxons (*c.* 880–899)
Edward the Elder, king of the Anglo-Saxons (899–924)

East Anglia

Edmund, king of East Anglia (855–869)
Æthelred and Oswald [as puppets of the Danes] (*c.* 875)

DANISH RULERS

Guthrum [Athelstan] (*c.* 880–890)
Eohric (*c.* 890–902) with Æthelwold from 900–902. Both killed at the battle of the Holm.

Northumbria

ENGLISH RULERS

    Osberht (*c.* 848–*c.* 863)
    Ælle (*c.* 863–867)
    Osberht [restored] (867)
    Ecgberht [as puppet of the Danes] (867–*c.* 872)

DANISH RULERS

    Ricsige [as puppet of the Danes] (872/3–876)
    Halfdan I (mid-870s–877)
    Ecgberht II [as puppet of the Danes] (876–*c.* 878)
    Guthfrith I (883–895)
    Sigeferth (fl. *c.* 895)
    Cnut (fl. *c.* 895)
    Æthelwold [as champion of the Danes] (*c.* 900–902)
    Eowils and Halfdan II (*c.* 902–910)

Sources and Bibliography

Books on the Military Aspects of the Period

Abels, R., 1988, *Lordship and Military Obligation in Anglo-Saxon England*, London, British Museum Press.

Abels, R., 1998, *Alfred the Great: War, Kingship and Culture in Anglo-Saxon England*, New York, Longman.

Hill, P., 2004, *The Age of Athelstan: Britain's Forgotten History*, Stroud, Tempus.

Hollister, C. Warren, 1962, *Anglo-Saxon Military Institutions on the Eve of the Norman Conquest*, Oxford, The Clarendon Press.

Loyn, H., 1994, *The Vikings in Britain*, Oxford, Blackwell.

McGrail, S. (ed.), 1990, *Maritime Celts, Frisians and Saxons*, London.

Peddie, J., 1989, *Alfred, Warrior King*, Stroud, Sutton.

Pollard, J., 2005, *Alfred the Great: the Man who Made England*, London, John Murray.

Sawyer, P., 1982, *Kings and Vikings*, London, Methuen.

Smyth, A.P., 1977, *Scandinavian Kings in the British Isles 850–880*, Oxford.

Smyth, A.P., 1987, *Scandinavian York and Dublin*, Dublin.

Stenton, Sir F., 1971, *Anglo-Saxon England*, Oxford.

Sturdy, D., 1995, *Alfred the Great*, London, Constable.

Ancient Texts and Other Sources

Bell, A. (ed.), 1960, *L'Estoire des Engleis* (Gaimar), Oxford.

Campbell, A. (ed.), 1962, *The Chronicle of Æthelweard*, Nelson's Medieval Texts, London.

Sources and Bibliography

Dumville and Lapidge (eds), 1984, *Annals of St Neots. The Anglo-Saxon Chronicle: A Collaborative Edition, 17*, Cambridge.

Keynes, S. and Lapidge, M. (eds), 1983, *Alfred the Great. Asser's Life of Alfred and Other Contemporary Sources*, London, Penguin Books.

Nelson, J.L. (ed.), 1991, *Annals of St Bertin*, Manchester.

Swanton, M., 1996, *The Anglo-Saxon Chronicle*, J.M. Dent, London.

Collections of Papers

Graham-Campbell, J., Hall, R., Jesch, J. and Parsons N. (eds), *Vikings and the Danelaw: Selected Papers from the Thirteenth Viking Conference*, Oxford, Oxbow.

Reuter, T. (ed.), 2003, *Alfred the Great: Papers from the Eleventh-Centenary Conferences*, proceedings of conferences held in 1999 in London and Southampton.

Single Papers

Beavan, M.L.R., 1917, 'The Regnal Dates of Alfred, Edward the Elder and Athelstan', *English Historical Review*, pp. 517–31.

Binns, A., 1981, 'The Ships of the Vikings, were they "Viking ships"?' *Proceedings of the Eighth Viking Congress*, Ed. Bekker-Neilsen et al, Odense.

Brooks, N., 1971, 'The Development of Military Obligations in the Eighth and Ninth Centuries in England', in Clemoes, P. and Hughes, K. (eds), *England Before the Conquest*, Cambridge.

Clapham, J.H., 1910, 'The Horsing of the Danes', *English Historical Review*, Vol. 25, No. 98, pp. 287–93.

Davis, R.H.C., 1982, 'Alfred and Guthrum's Frontier', *English Historical Review*, Vol. 27, pp. 803–10.

Hassall, J.M. and Hill, D., 1970, 'Pont del'Arche: Frankish influence on the West Saxon burh?' *Archaeological Journal CXXVII*, pp. 188–95.

Hill, D., 1967, 'The Burghal Hidage–Lyng', *Proceedings of the Somerset Archaeological and Natural History Society CXI*, pp. 64–6.

Hill, P.R., 2000, 'The Nature and Function of Spearheads in England *c.* AD 700–1100', *Journal of the Arms and Armour Society, Vol. XVI, No. 5*, pp. 257–80.

Magoun, F.P., 1942, 'King Alfred's Naval and Beach Battle with the Danes in 896', *Modern Language Review XXXVII*, pp. 409–14.

Morgan Owen, T., 1874, 'The Battle of Buttington, with a brief Sketch of the Affairs of Powys and Mercia', *Montgomeryshire Collections 7*, p. 260.

Spurrell, F.C.J., 1890, 'Hæsten's Camps at Shoebury and Benfleet in Essex', *Essex Naturalist IV*, pp. 150–7.

Stenton, F. M., 1909, 'Æthelweard's Account of the Last Years of King Alfred's Reign', *English Historical Review XXIV*, pp. 79–84.

Stenton, F. M., 1912, 'The Danes at Thorney Island in 893', *English Historical Review XXVII*, pp. 512–13.

Whitbread, L., 'Æthelweard and the Anglo-Saxon Chronicle', *English Historical Review LXXIV*, pp. 577–89.

Index

The Viking Wars of Alfred the Great

Index